A GARDEN
BEYOND
PARADISE

A GARDEN BEYOND PARADISE

THE MYSTICAL POETRY
OF RUMI

JONATHAN STAR
AND
SHAHRAM SHIVA

BANTAM BOOKS
NEW YORK   TORONTO   LONDON   SYDNEY   AUCKLAND

A GARDEN BEYOND PARADISE

A Bantam Book / December 1992

Library of Congress Cataloging-in-Publication Data

Jalāl al-Dīn al-Rūmī, Maulana, 1207–1273.
A garden beyond paradise : the mystical poetry of Rumi / [edited
by] Jonathan Star and Shahram Shiva.
p.   cm.
Includes bibliographical references.
ISBN 0-553-37104-5 (pbk)
1. Jalāl al-Dīn al-Rūmī, Maulana, 1207–1273—Translations into
English. I. Star, Jonathan. II. Shiva, Shahram. III. Title.
PK6480.E5S73   1992   92-13635
891'.5511—dc20   CIP

*To obtain more information about this book, or about activities concerning Rumi
and Sufism, please write to:*
FRIENDS OF RUMI, 26 White Pine Lane,
Princeton, New Jersey, 08540.

Published simultaneously in the United States and Canada

PRINTED IN THE UNITED STATES OF AMERICA

RRH   0 9 8 7 6 5 4 3 2 1

To
our
Beloved.

Wait till you look within yourself
and see what is there.
O seeker,
One leaf in that Garden
is worth more than all of Paradise!

— *Rumi*

CONTENTS

INTRODUCTION

Nowhere have the impulses of Eastern and Western spirituality been more vividly expressed than in the works of the Sufi saint, Jalaluddin Rumi. His poetry is a boundless fusion of all time and cultures, all mysteries, and all truths; his every word came from a place of love and inspiration, a place where the soul and its Creator are one. During his lifetime, Muslims, Jews, and Christians were inspired by his company and found that his teachings illumined the spiritual truths of their own faith. To this day, seven centuries after his death, people are still illumined by his spirit, for they can't help but see some aspect of themselves revealed, some secret longing laid bare, or some hidden feeling perfectly expressed. By capturing the spiritual pulse of his own age, Rumi has captured every age; by revealing the ecstasy of his own heart, he has come to touch every heart.

Rumi was born in Balkh (present-day Afghanistan), on the far eastern border of the Persian Empire, and lovingly called Jalaluddin ("Glory of the faith"). Balkh was a thriving center of Islamic learning, a Buddhist capital, and a place near the Silk Road where a rich exchange of goods and ideas took place. Rumi's family enjoyed great prestige there; his father, Baha Walad, was a renowned scholar and Sufi adept. In 1219, as the Mongol armies of Ghengis Khan neared the city, Baha Walad, with his family and disciples, fled to the Western part of the empire. The next year the Mongol armies utterly destroyed every city in the region, including Balkh. According to one account: "fourteen thousand copies of the Koran were destroyed, fifteen thousand students and professors were slain, and two hundred thousand adult males were led outside the city and shot to death with arrows."

After nine years of traveling, Rumi's family headed toward the Seljuk Empire (present-day Turkey) where many theologians, scholars, and artists found refuge during this troubled time. When the Seljuk King heard about Baha Walad and his family he invited them to stay in the capital city of Konya. (The name Rumi—which is popular only in the West—comes from *Rum* since Konya lay in the direction of Rome.) The king received them with great honor, and put Baha Walad in charge of a newly constructed *madrasa* (college) in the center of the city. Rumi, still under his father's tutelage, continued to study the disciplines of his heritage. By age twenty-four he was an acknowledged master of Arabic grammar, principles of Islamic law, Koranic commentary, theology, math, astronomy, and Sufi lore. A few years after arriving in Konya, Baha Walad died and Rumi took over his father's position as head of the college. The talented youth taught with great pomp and flair, unraveling the most complex and baffling problems of theology. He became the spiritual guide for thousands of disciples, including the king, and everyone called him *Maulana,* "Our Master." Despite all his genius and accomplishments, Rumi was not complete: he lacked a direct experience of the Supreme Reality, that one the Sufis call "the Beloved." Intellectually, Rumi knew everything about the mysterious "wine" of Sufism—he knew what it looked like, what it smelled like, where it came from, how to prepare it, and even how to teach it to others—but he had never *tasted* it himself! One afternoon in 1244 all this changed—Rumi met his Master, Shams-e Tabriz, who gave him that divine taste, that direct experience of God, which transformed his life completely.

This historic meeting is often described, with the Koranic line, as "the meeting of two oceans." Several accounts of this event have been recorded, and though each differs in specifics, they all tell of an upheaval in Rumi and his sudden realization that all his book-knowledge was worthless when compared to the experience of the "unseen world" that only Shams could give him. Rumi's son, Sultan Walad writes: "On account of Maulana's (Rumi's) purity and faith, he was singled out by God, who revealed His Face (true form) and allowed him all the benefits and blessings of this special favor. After years of longing he saw God's Face and all the secrets of the universe opened up before him. He saw what could not be seen; he heard what was never heard before. Shams showed him that ocean of love: Maulana dove in and was gone forever."

Some flame, some mysterious and divine force, had passed from Shams to Rumi. Commenting on this phenomenon, the French scholar, Eva de Vitray-Meyerovitch, writes: "It is not only the teaching of a method [that brings about this transformation] . . . but an initiatic transmission, the communication of a spiritual influence, a divine influx (*baraka*)." Yogic scriptures call this "divine influx," or awakening of spiritual energy, *Shaktipat,* and have always considered it to be the first step on the journey toward realization of God. This awakening is an essential, yet highly secretive, element in all spiritual traditions. In the yogic text, *Devatma Shakti,* one manifestation of this awakened energy is described, which is strikingly reminiscent of Rumi's and could even be applied to the Prophet Mohammed who while receiving revelations from God would shiver, tremble, cry out in strange voices, and hear bell-like sounds:

> If you sit for prayers and your body begins to shake, and in ec-
> stasy you begin to sing hymns in tones of music charming to the
> ear, and whose composition and poetry come out spontaneously;
> if your hands take on a rhythmical clapping, and you pronounce
> words you don't know, but the sound pulses with ecstasy in
> your mind, know that the supreme energy, *kundalini,* has been
> awakened in you.

Rumi's life blossomed in the hands of his master: all his previous practices bore fruit, all his knowledge was refined, and all the mysteries of the universe were revealed to him. But these halcyon days were brief: After being in Konya for only sixteen months, Shams disappeared, without a word. Ahmed al Aflaki, a disciple of Rumi's grandson, gave this account of what followed:

When Rumi heard the news he was heartbroken and could not sleep at night. One morning, in the wee hours, he drifted off to sleep and dreamt that Shams was sitting with a young Frenchman in a small tavern on the outskirts of Damascus. They were gambling. With each throw of the dice, Shams won more and more of the young man's money until the poor fellow's pouch was completely empty. At this, the Frenchman jumped up and struck Shams across the face.

Rumi suddenly awoke from his dream. He called for his son, Sultan Walad, and said, "Go to Damascus, to a small tavern at the base of the Salihiyye Mountains. There you will find Shams playing dice in a small tavern. Take this gold and silver, put it in his shoes, turn them toward Konya, and implore him to return to us."

Faithful to his father's instructions, Sultan Walad, along with twenty other disciples, set out for Damascus. When they arrived at the tavern, they found Shams exactly as Rumi had described—he was being beaten and insulted by a young Frenchman. Sultan Walad fell at Sham's feet, poured sacks of gold and silver into his slippers, and begged him, in his father's name, to return home. The twenty disciples bowed in turn, asking Shams to forgive them and anyone else who might have treated him disrespectfully. They too asked him to return.

On seeing this, the young Frenchman realized he had insulted a great master. He was ashamed and humbled. He then knelt in front of Shams, offered him all his remaining possessions, and implored Shams to accept him as a disciple. Shams refused, saying: "Go back to Europe. Visit the seekers there, be the leader of their gathering, and remember us in your prayers."

Shams agreed to return to Konya, and Sultan Walad brought him a horse to ride on. Shams told Sultan Walad to ride on the horse but he refused, saying: "The king should walk and the servant should ride?—Never!" And Sultan Walad ran besides the stirrups of Shams's horse all the way back to Konya.

After the joyous reunion of Shams and Rumi, Shams said: "There are two things I received from God: my wisdom and a pure heart. I have given my wisdom to you, and to your son I have given a pure heart. Even if Sultan Walad spent a thousand years on this path, it would never be equal in merit to what he received from me on his trip to Damascus."

Once again Rumi enjoyed the ecstatic company of Shams—the long retreats, the nights of chanting and prayer. Once again he became totally immersed in the love for his master. And once again Shams disappeared—this time never to return. For two years Rumi searched and searched, but in vain. When he arrived back in Konya he was devastated with grief. With Shams gone a part of Rumi was gone. To fill the emptiness, Rumi began to sing and dance and recite poetry. In his heart, Rumi discovered that he and Shams were one.

With a unique sympathy, the whole of Konya followed Rumi's transformation. They saw him enter the city as a youth with his distinguished father. They watched as he became a prized scholar and an eloquent interpreter of Islamic theology. They saw him meet Shams, and looked on in bewilderment as he gave up his mantle, assumed the cloth of a Sufi, and began singing and dancing in complete abandon. And when his master disappeared, they saw his painful longing find expression in poetry—poetry that was exquisite, poetry that would change the heart of the Muslim world forever.

Rumi spent the rest of his life in Konya, devoting his time

to spiritual practice, teaching, and writing. The fruits of his efforts were two masterpieces: the *Divan-e Shams-e Tabrizi,* a voluminous rhapsody of divine love poems; and the *Mathnawi,* a classic telling of thousands of stories and parables which, because of its profound impact, has often been called "the Koran of the Persian language." Rumi also served as the spiritual guide for thousands of people and formed the Mevlevi Brotherhood of Whirling Darveshes, which has always embodied the traits of his personality: humility, compassion, and love for one's neighbor.

The thirteenth century was an age of great chaos and brutality; it was a time of profound conflicts and irreversible movements that put the whole of Islam under siege. From the West came the onslaught of the Crusades who were determined to wrest back the Holy Land from the Arabs. From the East came the unstoppable Mogul armies who were ruthlessly destroying every trace of Islamic culture. Internally, there was dissension and moral decay. But behind this outer gloom there were rays of hope, and eminent religious figures of every tradition were emerging. In Central Europe, Thomas Aquinas, Saint Francis, and Meister Eckhart were spreading the gospel of Jesus; in Spain, Moses de Leon and Maimonides were laying the foundation of Jewish theology and mysticism. Sweeping through all of North India was a devotional movement called Bhakti, headed by Namdev and the "King of Saints" Jnaneshwar Maharaj. And the distant land of Japan saw the birth of Dogen, who was considered the greatest of all Zen Masters. Islam was also blessed during this age with its most famous and influential Sufi masters, such as Ibn Arabi, Fariduddin Attar, Mahmud Shabestari, Amir Khusrau, and Fakhruddin Araqi.

The thirteenth century not only marked the start of Europe's Renaissance but the high-point of Islamic culture—it was the Golden Age of its poetic and spiritual life, with Rumi as its crowning glory. By this time all the major treatises of

Islam and Sufism had been written and every religious question had been resolved. Islamic theology and Sufism found its perfect balance in the writings of al Ghazalli (d. 1111). The influence of Greek thought on Islam found masterful treatment in the works of Averros (1126–1198). The theory of man's inseparable Unity with God was fully developed by Ibn Arabi (1165–1240), and the two great *Mathnawi* (rhyming couplet) writers, Sana'i (d. 1133) and Attar (?1140–?1220), had completed their epics. Rumi was heir to this immense intellectual and spiritual fortune. His peerless achievement is not marked by the system of theology he put forth—he offered none—but in the masterful way he recast, in the light of his own experience, all the knowledge he had inherited. His own psyche became a crucible into which he poured the wisdom of his age; and there, boiling in the depths of his own soul, fueled by his intense longing for God, the whole of Sufism found its perfect expression.

Sufism is the name given to the various mystical sects of Islam that honor love and devotion for God above all else. The Sufis seek the "hidden mysteries" of life; they yearn for a direct experience of God, the one they call "the Beloved." The Sufis do not view the Beloved as a harsh master or an unreachable Absolute. Rather, the Beloved is approached with total love, with no boundaries, and with all the excitement that might accompany the love one has for a human beloved. The Sufis' unabashed love for God caused them to dance and sing and celebrate long into the night. By conventional standards they were crazy and people often called them mad—but at the same time, these mad Sufis were acknowledged as the greatest artists, poets, and mystics of Islam.

Sufism first emerged in Baghdad during the eighth and ninth centuries, and was blessed by such great saints as Rabi'a of Basra, Bayazid Bestami, and Mansur al Hallaj. It took on the color of Islamic culture and was shaped by many traditions but one could rightly say that the essence of Sufism existed for as long as the soul has yearned to join its Creator. The impeccable scholar R. A. Nicholson writes: "All manifestations of the mystical spirit are fundamentally the same, and we shall not be astonished to encounter in remote lands and different ages of the world 'one set of principles variously combined.' " In Sufism, perhaps more than any other mystical tradition, this one principle takes many different forms and appears through a kaleidoscope of religious practices and philosophies. Sufism has shades of early Greek thought, including that of Plato, Aristotle, and especially Plotinus (known as Shaykh al Yaunani—"The Greek Master"). Its practice includes the use of rosaries—common to Buddhism and other traditions; the keeping of vigils, vows of silence, and the wearing of woolen robes, which is common among the Christians. The continual repetition of God's Name, deification of the master, and the proclamation of one's unity with God is similar to that of the Hindus. And of course Sufi doctrine conforms with both the central tenet of Islam (that God is one, Omnipotent, and without equal) and with the teachings found in the Koran, which contains many stories from the Old and New Testaments, including those of Joseph, Abraham, Moses, Jesus, and Mary. In the Koran, however, these stories have been condensed and differ slightly from the Judeo-Christian versions. For example, Jesus is regarded as a prophet, and called "the Spirit of God" [43:61], but he does not hold a special status as Savior or Redeemer, nor does his life end on the cross. [4:157].

The first Sufis engaged in ascetic practices similar to the early Christian monks. In Islam, however, there are no monasteries, and the Prophet—who himself had eight wives—called on men to participate in society. The ideal Sufi does not celebrate life by withdrawing from the world but by a total participation in it, by seeing everything and everyone as an aspect of God. He lives by the Koranic line "To God belongs the East and the West; in whatever direction you turn to look, there is the Face of God." The Sufi saint Abu Sa'id (d. 1049) practiced severe austerities for many years (one of which included repeating the entire Koran every night while suspended upside down!) but in the end he realized that God was everywhere and could be attained in the midst of one's daily life. He wrote:

> If people want to draw God near, they must seek Him in the hearts of others. They must speak to everyone, whether they are present or absent; and if they desire to be the light which guides others, then like the Sun, they must show the same face to all. Bringing joy to a single heart is better than building a thousand holy shrines. Enslaving one soul with love, is better than setting free a thousand captives.
>
> The (true saint) lives in the midst of other people. He rises in the morning; he eats and sleeps when needed. He buys and sells in the marketplace just like everyone else. He marries, has children, and meets with his friends, yet never for an instant does he forget God.

Before the introduction of Sufism, Persian poetry was rather lifeless. Odes did little more than praise rich dignitaries or the military exploits of rulers; lyrical works made no attempt to convey feelings, emotions, or spiritual insights. Sufism marked a new beginning: poetry became a venue for the expression of ecstatic revelation and divine love; it became a living force that inspired a state of ecstasy in all who heard it.

The first mystics of Islam soon realized the severe limitations of the existing language and began to alter its form to voice their ineffable inner experience. In the ninth century, the Sufis of Baghdad reshaped the images and simple phrases of Arabic love songs to tell about their ecstasy, their insights, and about the path of divine love. Two centuries later with the poetry of San'ai (d. 1150) Sufi theology found its full range of poetic expression. In his writings he employed every verse form and meter, including *ghazals* (love poems), *ruba'i* (quatrains), and the long rhyming couplet form known as *Mathnawi*.

Within this new poetic form, the Sufis created a language of symbolism to describe the soul's divine longing and the ecstasy of union with God. The Sufi poets portrayed the soul as a distraught maiden pining for her beloved. In the verses of Rumi especially, the soul cries with the wailing song of the reed-flute, longing for the reed-bed from which it was cut. Sometimes the soul is portrayed as a helpless bird looking for its nest; a tender flower waiting for the breeze of Spring; a fish in search of the ocean; a pawn with its heart set on becoming a king.

Perhaps the most surprising and most often misunderstood metaphors used by the Sufis are those which employ the images of wine, taverns, and drunkenness. With a simple reading, this poetry could be mistaken as wanton sensuality and recklessness. Actually these images are all metaphors to express a divine intoxication. In this barroom language, God is called the *Saaqi* (the Cupbearer); the nectar of God's love is "wine," and losing oneself in the Beloved is "becoming totally drunk." This debauched symbolism had a special appeal for the Sufis because wine was forbidden in Islam yet promised in Paradise. R. A. Nicholson writes: "This erotic and bacchanalian symbolism is not, of course, peculiar to the mystical poetry of Islam, but nowhere else is it displayed so opulently and in such perfection."

In Sufi poetry the Beloved is everything and everyone: Sometimes soothing the soul, at other times tormenting it. As the Cupbearer, She is sweet and beautiful; as the "Friend" He is playful and jovial; as the Heart-Ravishing Beloved, She appears ruthless, indifferent, and even cruel. The frequent use of images that involve killing, alleyways flowing with blood, cauldrons filled with bodies, and heads stacked on the floor, may seem alien and shocking to the average reader—certainly not the stuff of a love poem! To the Sufis, however, this torment is a sign of God's compassion: It is the destruction of man's limited ego, and part of God's divine preparation that ultimately makes the soul perfect. Rumi compares this "torment" in the hands of the Beloved to the boiling of chickpeas.

Look at the chickpeas in the pot and how they keep jumping up when put on the fire.

At every moment the chickpeas boil, they come to the top and raise their voices with a hundred cries:

"Why are you torturing us with this fire? You found us appealing, and you paid for us, why do you now treat us with such contempt?

The housewife keeps pushing them down with the ladle: "Now, now!" she says, "Boil nicely and don't run from the one who made the fire.

I do not cook you out of spite; it is only so you may gain taste and flavor . . ."

The chickpeas reply, "Since this is the case, O lady, we will boil with delight—give us your blessings!

In this boiling, you play the part of our Creator. Stir us with your spoon, for your stirring is our salvation!

We are like elephants: beat us on the head so we will not dream about India or its gardens,

So that we may surrender ourselves to the boiling and come upon the embrace of our Beloved."

A generation before Rumi, Fariduddin Attar completed his *Parliament of the Birds,* a long rhyming poem about a flock of birds who set out for a distant land to find their King Bird. In the end thirty birds arrive, only to discover that the King they long sought, called the *Simorgh,* was none other than themselves, *Simorgh* meaning *Si* (thirty) + *morgh* (birds). Following Attar, this avian symbolism became a large part of the Sufi language: The soul becomes a *nightingale* in search of a perfect rose. Words of the spirit, which cannot be reached from earth, are called "the language of the birds." And the "Great Bird" symbolizes the transcendent spirit of God. For Rumi, this symbolism was especially dear because Shams—who was known to travel a great deal—was nicknamed *Piranda,* the Bird.

Like the wandering of the soul, or the tireless flight of birds,

Rumi's poetry is always moving. It tells of the all-encompassing movement of life: the rising and setting sun, the change of seasons, the turning of the night sky, and the whirling of man which embodies all the movements of heaven and earth. Rumi often composed his poetry while whirling, and the inherent structure of his poetry—the relentless flow of imagery, the inner cadence, and the mantra-like repetition of rhymes—often echoes this whirling motion. There are also subtle movements from one level of meaning to another, and from one perspective to another. Even the state of silence that Rumi refers to so often is not stagnant but filled with ever-new possibilities. Nothing with Rumi can be taken literally: one must always be aware of the meaning behind the meaning, and the veils behind the veils.

At the deepest level of Rumi's poetry, however, he tells only one story: the soul's search for the Beloved. Every allegory is about this search, and every symbol represents some aspect of the Beloved. Even Rumi's use of his master's name, "Shams," "Shamsuddin," or "Shams-e Tabriz," is not so much a literal reference to his master but a symbol—a very personal and immediate symbol—representing the formless Beloved.

The more one reads Rumi, the more apparent his genius becomes. However, what has earned him the title of "the greatest mystical poet of any age" is not his poetic brilliance, or his "triumphant mastery of language," but the way he has infused his imagery and his language with the power of his own experience and the fire of his own longing. The spring he speaks of may represent union with God, but for Rumi it becomes a resurrection, a thousand meadows bursting with color. The Sun may represent divine illumination, but every day that it rose, it was the refulgence of Rumi's very soul. And the Beloved about whom he wrote with such passion was no mere symbol: it was a living presence within him, fired by the real human longing he had for his own master. The poetry of Rumi will forever be a phenomenon. He, like no one else, has taken life and made it divine; he has taken one vision and made it universal; he has taken all of God's glory and made it his own—but more than this, he has made it our own. He writes:

Come, come! For *you* are the one who bestows glory and beauty.
Come, come! For *you* are the cure of a thousand sorrows.
Come, come! Even though you have never left—
    Come and hear some poetry.

Sit in the place of my soul,
    for you are a thousand souls of mine.
Begone with your lovers and ancient longings,
    for *you* are the Beloved!

According to the Sufi saint Abdurrahman Jami, Shams and the poet Araqi, both stayed with Shaykh Baba Hemal. Every day Araqi would relate his spiritual insights in the most beautiful poetry. One day the Shaykh said to Shams: "The secrets and experience of the unseen world are revealed to your brother Araqi—is nothing revealed to you?"

Shams replied: "I know secrets that are held back even from Araqi, but I do not have the words in which to clothe them."

Baba Hemal replied: "God will bring you a disciple who will tell the world the entire truth from the beginning to the end; he will clothe it in the most beautiful words and sounds, and put them in your name."

That truth, "from the beginning to the end," is the *Divan-e Shams-e Tabrizi* ("The work of Shams Tabriz"), a collection of some 2000 quatrains and 3400 odes from which all the poems in this book were selected. The *Divan* can be read like a map of the spiritual journey: it is filled with the light of Rumi's divine state and charts the whole range of experience and emotion that a seeker might encounter on his journey to the Beloved.

The first attempts to translate Rumi's poetry into English were made at the beginning of the century by British scholars, who produced diligent and precise works and, by their own admission, with "minimal concession to readability." Contemporary American scholars, acting with more sensitivity to the reader, have offered a group of impressive and readable translations. A number of poetic versions have also re-translated Rumi into a more modern and familiar language. Though these works have helped us, and inspired us, none of them truly voices *our* feelings for Rumi or captures our connection to the "spirit" of his poetry. Thus, this work is our offering, our attempt to bring out Rumi's spirit—as we see it—and to convey it as fully and convincingly as language permits.

Rumi was both a Persian poet and a mystical poet. As with all Persian poets of his time, his verses adhered to a particular form and stucture. The quatrain (*ruba'i*) he used consisted of four, equal-length hemistiches (half-lines), with the first, second, and fourth rhyming. The ode (*ghazal*) was structured like the quatrain, with the first, second, and fourth hemistiches rhyming—after that, every other hemistich rhymes.

A_____   A_____

A_____   B(A)_____

(QUATRAIN)

A_____   A_____

A_____   B_____

A_____   C_____

A_____   D_____

E_____   E_____

(ODE)

All attempts to duplicate the Persian rhyme scheme and meter in English have proven impossible without an intolerable distortion to the sense of the original—thus we have abandoned that approach. Here we have tried to give the sense of the Persian by using an English style which is terse, cadent, and whose structure gives some sense of the repetitive and breathless urgency so characteristic of Rumi's original.

Rumi was not only a Persian poet but a poet-saint. He sang about divine states and spiritual experiences that transcended language and culture, and often departed from the text by adding a connecting line, shifting around an image, or recasting an idea into poetic paraphrase. In the end, our goal has been to make these poems *his*—to translate them in such a way that they sound like Rumi, feel like Rumi, and could have come from Rumi's lips were he here, among us, singing his sublime verses in our mother tongue.

JONATHAN STAR

We would like to thank all those people whose time and efforts have added to this work: Our thanks go to R. A. Nicholson, B. Z. Furuzanfar, and all the authors upon whose works we have relied; to George Franklin for his comments on the finished poetry; to William Chittick, Orrin Star, Patrick Tierney, and Swami Anantananda for giving their feedback on the introduction; to Javad Ibn Assad Allah and Khanum Naz Zar; and to all the Sufi saints whose ecstatic verses have been a never-ending source of inspiration.

QUATRAINS

THE BELOVED

The Sufis do not view God as some harsh and distant master, but rather as their most intimate and cherished companion. Endearingly, they call themselves "lovers," and the God they seek, "the Beloved." All a Sufi strives for, all he reaches for, all he ever wants is the Beloved. This unswerving love causes him to see the form of his Beloved everywhere: as pure beauty and pure love, as the master and the playful "Friend," as the vibrant, living presence that permeates every aspect of life.

O my Beloved!
Take me,
Liberate my soul,
Fill me with your love,
 and release me from both worlds.

If I set my heart
On anything but you,
O fire, burn me from inside!

O my Beloved
Take away what I want,
Take away what I do,
Take away everything
 that takes me from you.

I know nothing of two worlds—
All I know is the One—
  I seek only One,
  I know only One,
  I find only One,
And I sing of only One.

I am so drunk
On the wine of my Beloved
    that both worlds
Have slipped from my reach.

Now I have no business here
    but to reach
For the cup of my Beloved.

The Lover is ever drunk with love;
    He is free, he is mad,
He dances with ecstasy and delight.

Caught by our own thoughts,
    we worry about every little thing,
But once we get drunk on that love,
Whatever will be, will be.

My eyes see only the face of the Beloved.
What a glorious sight,
    for that sight is beloved.
Why speak of two?—
The Beloved is in the sight,
    and the sight is in the Beloved.

A whale lives for the ocean,
A panther lives for the forest,
    The miser lives for wealth,
    The lover lives for a sight of his Beloved.

His sweet water cleansed my soul
and removed its every sorrow.
Now we are joined in perfect union.

They say love opens a door
from one heart to another;
But if there is no wall
how can there be a door?

When *you* dance
the whole universe dances.
What a wonder,
I've looked
and now I cannot look away!
Take me or do not take me,
both are the same—
As long as there is life in this body,
I am your servant.

O how the Beloved fits inside my heart—
Like a thousand souls in one body,
A thousand harvests in one sheaf of wheat,
A thousand whirling heavens
        in the eye of a needle.

I plant some flowers without you,
        they become thorns.
I see a peacock, it turns into a snake.
I play the *rubaab**—nothing but noise.
I go to the highest heaven, it's a burning hell.

* A high-pitched string instrument played with a bow.

In one sweet moment,
        She burst from my heart.
There we sat on the floor,
        drinking ruby wine.
Trapped by Her beauty,
        I saw and I touched—
My whole face became eyes,
All my eyes became hands.

My heart is the *rubaab*, your love the bow.
My soul weeps quietly
        as you play me your song.

Play on, my Beloved!
Let me not miss one note of your melody
        nor one beat of your heart.

Faithless is the one who doesn't rejoice when you do.
Dead is the one who doesn't dance when you do.
Wisest in all the world is a fool
    if he doesn't tear his heart open when you do.

If I pray
    it's only so my heart might turn toward you.
If I face the Ka'be
    it's only so my eyes might turn toward you.
Otherwise,
    I'll rid the world of prayer,
    I'll tear down the Ka'be.*

* The most sacred shrine of Islam, located at Mecca.

They say it's night,
      but I don't know about day and night—
I only know the face of that one
      who fills the heavens with light.

O night, you are dark because
      you do not know Him.
O day, go and learn from Him
      what it means to shine.

O my Beloved,
The thought of you keeps me from you.
The thought of your face covers your face.

When I remember your lips,
      they fade away.
When I think of your kisses
      they come no more.

Your love has filled me
    with a madness
    no one could ever know.

Your gaze has enchanted my heart
    with a poem
    no one could ever write.

I was with Him last night,
    that one who raises my soul to heaven.

    All I did was pray and beg.
    All he did was turn his head and smile.

The night was over before our story ended.
But it's not the night's fault—
    this game's been going on a long time.

The lover came, full of despair—
    I can say no more.
His manner was bold and fiery—
    I can say no more.
The Beloved said, *Don't.*
The lover said, *I won't.*

Then both looked up and smiled—
    I can say no more.

The Beloved looked at me
With compassion and said,
    How can you go on living without me?
I said, *I swear, like a fish out of water.*
He said, *Then why do you hold so tight
    to the dry land?*

To that Beloved,
　　　flower and thorn are one;
A verse of the Koran
And a Brahmin's thread are one.

Don't try to impress Him—
To that Beloved,
　　　hero and fool are one.

I recited a verse,
　　　the Lover laughed.
He said, *Are you trying to hold me*
　　　in your cute little rhyme?
I said, *You didn't have to break it to pieces.*
He said, *It was too small!*
　　　I couldn't fit in it.
　　　That's why it broke to pieces.

I swallowed some of His sweet wine
    and now I'm ill—
    my chest aches, my fever is high.

The doctor says, *Take these pills.*
    OK, time to take these pills.
The doctor says, *Drink this tea.*
    OK, time to drink this tea.
The doctor says, *Get rid of the sweet wine of his lips.*
    OK, time to get rid of the doctor.

If I die, lay me next to the Beloved.

If He looks at me, don't be surprised.
If He kisses me on the lips, don't be surprised.
If I open my eyes and smile, don't be surprised.

Your love is my reason,
    the resting place of my soul.

I said, *I'll leave you alone for two or three days—*
But I couldn't. O my Beloved,
How can I ever hold this love from you?

    I'm crazy, I'm a total mess—
Take my hand.
I'm empty, I just can't find myself—
Take my hand.

This world is full of crooked pots,
Each with a lid to fit.
But look at me, I'm lost, I have no one—
Take my hand.

I am waving a scarf
     below your window—
Do you think I'm waving for you?
No, no,
Go, go—
It's not for you.
I just happen to be waving a scarf
     below your window.

I see the moon—
     it doesn't need to be full.
I see the moon—
     it doesn't need to rise.

He is the water of life.
Oh what a moon I see
     reflected in *His* water!

The soft light of the moon
        looks like you.
The tender wings of an angel
        look like you—
No, no—
What am I saying?
Only You look like You.

Look at Him,
        flushed red like a little girl!
Oh what pain I'd have
        if someone were to cover my eyes.

In the reflection of His face
        all the beauty of heaven shines.
Without Him,
        there is only mud.

I have grown old,
      but not old from the days.
I have grown old
      but not old from the smiles and games
      of my Beloved.

With every breath
      I am baked and unbaked,
With every step
      I become the trap
      and the one who takes the bait.

You call me an *Infidel*.
You call me *Old, young, a newborn.*
When I leave this world,
      don't call me *Dead*.
Say rather, he *was* dead,
      then suddenly he came to life
      and ran off with the Beloved.

One glimpse of the Beloved was like alchemy—
He turned my copper soul into gold.

I searched for him with a thousand hands—
He reached out and grabbed me by the feet.

I am safe and warm
Under the Lover's blanket,
Yet keep thinking
He does not love me.
Surely if he heard my foolish thoughts—
Hidden, hidden,
Sweet, sweet—
He would laugh and laugh.

I warned my heart—
> *Stay away,*
> *He'll bring you only sorrow,*
> *He's bitter,*
> *He doesn't want you. . . .*
My heart laughed and said:
> *Since when*
> *is the taste of sugar bitter?*

At times I call him *Wine,*
At times, *Cup,*
At times, *Fire,*
At times, *Gold,*
At times *the Seed,* at times *the Plant,*
At times *the Hunt,* at times *the Trap.*

All this remains a mystery
Until I call him by his name.

Last night he was in a crowd,
    and I could not take him openly in my arms.
So I put my face next to his,
As if whispering a secret in his ear.

All the happiness in the world
    could not ease this longing.
There is only one cure—the Beloved.

I thought, "When I see him
    how much I will say!"
I saw Him and not a word came out.

I entered the Sacred City,
And took an oath of loyalty;
Wearing a white pilgrim's garb,
I wrapped the Ka'be with cloth.

But the moment I saw your face
I broke every vow I ever made.

Some say, "Love combined with wisdom is the best."
Others say, "Discipline and regular practice is the best."
Oh these words are more precious than gold,
But my life offered to Shams-e Tabriz is the best.

THE SUFI PATH

The Sufi's book is not composed of ink and letters: it is naught but a heart white as snow. The scholar's provisions are the mark of the pen. What are the Sufi's provisions? The footprints of the saints.
                                                                —Rumi

In the thirteenth century, Sufism was a rich mixture of religious practices that included remembrance of the Divine presence, chanting God's Name, praying, keeping vigil, and acting with charity toward one's neighbor. But the zeal and total abandon with which they sought the Beloved—and the uncontainable love that surged within them—often caused the Sufis to look crazy and bizarre. Few people could see past their outer appearance to the inner ecstasy; few could hear the music to which they danced.

The Sufi saint, Abu Sa'id, once wrote: "The path of Sufism consists of taking one step—a step outside yourself toward God." This one essential step, which binds all Sufis together, is the step they take toward a Shaykh, or spiritual Master. In Sufism, the Shaykh is seen as God's representative on earth, as an embodiment of the Prophet himself; and he is the only one with the power and the authority to guide a seeker on the path to union with God.

The morning breeze has secrets to tell you,
　　Don't sleep.
It's a time of inquiry and prayer,
　　Don't sleep.

O people of this world,
From this moment to eternity,
That unlocked door is open,
　　Don't go to sleep.

　　Life without a master
　　　　is either deep sleep
　　　　or death in disguise.

　Beware! This path
　Is not safe to travel alone—
　　　the water is deadly,
　　　the poison is sweet.

Sit in the company of Saints
    till they douse the smoke of your restlessness.

They may look bizarre,
    but don't be fooled by appearances—
They know your every thought
    even before you do.

I pick up a stick,
    it becomes a lute in my hands.
I make a mistake,
    it turns out for the best.
They say, *Do not travel during the holy month.*
I set out—and find a priceless treasure.

This brotherhood
    is not about being high or low,
    smart or ignorant.
There is no special assembly, no grand discourse,
    no proper schooling required.
This brotherhood is more like a drunken party
    full of tricksters, fools, charlatans, and madmen.

O soul, it's time for war:
    Put on your armor,
    Banish your fear,
    Cut through the facade of this world.
O soul, don't slacken now—
    it'll just be another cat and mouse story.

Alas, don't tell me—
   The Sufis are lost.
Don't tell me—
   The Christians are lost,
   The infidels are lost.
Alas my brother, *you* are lost!
That is why everyone else seems lost!

How could sorrow take root in us,
   we who are filled with joy?

The earth bears the weight of every misery,
Holding it in her bosom
   like a planted seed.
But we have left this earth
   and all its hardship—

All we see is the ceiling of paradise.

The moon rises and we rise with it.
Those with nothing
        have nothing to hold them down.

The whirling darveshes ask,
        Why are the wise ones so somber?
The wise ones ask,
        Why are the darveshes so mad?

We have burned all trace of work and profession;
We have nothing but poetry and love songs now.

We sing of heart, soul, and the Beloved—
Only to burn all trace
        of heart, soul, and Beloved.

You claim skill in every art
    and knowledge of every science,
Yet you cannot even hear
    what your own heart is telling you.

Until you can hear that simple voice
    How can you be a keeper of secrets?
    How can you be a traveller on this path?

How could sorrow approach the heart
    of a true lover?
Sorrow belongs to those
    who are dreary and alone.

The lover's heart
    is filled with an ocean,
And in its rolling waves
    the cosmos gently turn.

The face of that angel
     landed in my heart.
Is there anyone as happy as me?—
I truly cannot say.

I hear about sorrow
But have no idea what it is.

I laugh and laugh—I don't know why.

Only God knows why the stem of a flower
     quivers in the morning breeze.

How could sorrow stay with a true lover
    when he has a rubaab in his heart?

You say he looks crazy—
That's only because the music
    to which he dances
      is not tuned for your ears.

The darvesh who gives away
    the secret teachings, and all he owns,
    as freely as his own breath,
    doesn't need your scraps of bread.
That darvesh lives by the grace
    of someone else's hand.

Why cover yourself with the cloth of false prophets
    when the joy of a true master fills the world?

Why take bitter medicine for the ills of your heart
    when the sweet water of love fills the world?

If you want a pearl,
    Don't look for it in a puddle of water.
    Those who seek pearls
    Must dive into the deepest ocean.

And who will find the pearl?—
    Those who emerge
    From the waters of life
    Still thirsty.

The darvesh alone knows the secret of worship.
Piercing the infinite skies,
    he sees God and Master as one.

If you want to turn your rusty soul into gold,
Stay with the Master—
    He is the Alchemist.

Secretly we spoke,
    that wise one and me.
I said, *Tell me the secrets of the world.*
He said, *Sh . . . Let silence
Tell you the secrets of the world.*

DIVINE INTOXICATION

The first Sufis gathered in the lowly parts of the city, in a place called "the tavern" or "the ruins." There they would sing and dance in "drunken" ecstasy, calling out to the *Saaqi*, the Divine Cupbearer, yearning for the wine of love. This wild abandon gave these meetings the feel of a party or a brawl, and this is one reason why the metaphors of wine and drunkenness so aptly described the Sufis' divine intoxication. As Rumi makes explicit, however, this "drunkenness" was not the result of "wine from the grape" but of "wine" from God's love.

One way Rumi expressed his ecstasy—and one way he invoked it—was to whirl with music in the mystical dance known as *Sa'maa*. The images of music and dancing that infuse Rumi's poetry refer primarily to inner states and only secondly to the outer world. Symbolically, the *Sa'maa* represents a rebirth into spirit and man's inseparable unity with the cosmos—as man whirls, so do the heavens.

Who has ever seen such a mess?
The tavern of love is filled with drunkards!
Who has ever seen so many barrels
    shattered on the ground?
The floor and the ceiling of heaven
    are all splattered with wine!

But who has ever seen
    a cup of wine in anyone's hand?

We drink the wine of our own blood,
    aged in the barrels of our own souls.

We would give our lives for a sip of that nectar,
    our heads in exchange for one drop.

Another morning!
Pour the wine!
A life without his love
    is nothing but slow death.

It's up to you—
Accept the cry of the silent *rubaab*
Or endure this burning heart
    filled with grief.

O brother,
Take a sip from that golden cup—
Its nectar will turn this world into paradise.
Drink, drink, and laugh at the clown
    That others call despair.

I am so drunk
I have lost the way in
        and the way out.
I have lost the earth, the moon, and the sky!
Don't put another cup of wine in my hand,
        pour it in my mouth—
For I have lost the way to my mouth!

Our drunkenness does not come from wine.
The joy of our gathering
        does not come from the harp or rubaab.
With no celestial beauty to fill our cup,
Without friends, without singing, without wine,
We burst out like madmen,
        rolling drunk on the floor.

I'm in love:
          All your advice—what's the use?
I've drunk poison:
          All your sugar—what's the use?

They say *Hurry, tie his feet!*
But it's my heart that's gone crazy.
          All this rope around my feet—
          What's the use?

They say that paradise will be sublime
With jugs of precious wine
And plenty of damsels to fill our cups.

Why not drink that wine *now*?
Why not join the dance *now*?
For that's how it's going to be anyway.

O brother, bring the pure wine
    of love and freedom.

But master, a tornado is coming.

More wine!—
        we will teach this storm
        a thing or two about whirling!

Your dance just took me today
        and suddenly I began to whirl.
All the realms spun around me
        in endless celebration.
My soul lost its grip,
My body shed its fatigue.

Hearing your hands clap and your drum beat,
    I floated
            up to the heavens!

A hundred waves crash
    upon the waters of the heart,
Blown by the winds of *Sa'maa.**

Any heart that joins the water of all hearts
    will shatter in this wind
    and cry out *Sa'maa!*

The Sufi is dancing
    like the shimmering rays of the Sun,
Dancing from dusk till dawn.
They say, *This is the work of the Devil.*
Surely then, the Devil we dance with
    is sweet and joyous,
    and himself an ecstatic dancer!

* The whirling dance of the Sufis.

The world dances around the Sun.
The morning light breaks,
    Spinning up with delight.

How could anyone
Touched by your love
    Not dance like a weeping willow?

Today I spin wildly
    throughout the city;
I am the cup-bearer,
My head is the cup.

Perhaps a scholar will see me
    and drop his books.
Perhaps the world will see me
    and forget all its sorrow.

The Beloved, like the Sun, shine he will.
The lover, like the atoms, spin he will.
Like the breeze of Spring,
     Love sways the Earth gently—
Every branch, that is not dead, dance it will.

     A secret turns within my breast,
And with its turning
          the two worlds turn.

     I don't know head or feet,
Up or down—all is lost
          in this awesome turning.

TEACHINGS

Rumi's poetry is a direct appeal to the heart and the emotions yet it is filled with many practical teachings about life. He tells of the value of inner and outer silence, the need for good company, the ephemeral nature of this world (which he calls a "dustbowl"), the eternal process of growth and change, and the follies of blind faith.

For Rumi and the Sufis however, Love was the supreme teacher and the infallible means by which a soul could reach the Beloved. Cultivating love in the heart was considered the highest path, the one practice which embodied all other forms of worship and faith. According to the Sufis, this whole world came into existence for one reason—so that this Love could be known. Rumi writes:

> Love causes the ocean to boil like a cauldron,
> Love reduces the mountains to dust,
> Love splits the heavens into a hundred pieces,
> And without even knowing it,
> Love causes the earth to tremble.
> God said, "If not by pure love
> How could I have created this world?
> I have brought everything into existence,
> All the way up to the highest sphere,
> So you could know the glory of Love."

Don't think.
Don't get lost in your thoughts.
Your thoughts are a veil on the face of the Moon.
That Moon is your heart,
    and those thoughts cover your heart.
So let them go.
    Just let them fall into the water.

Without love,
    all worship is a burden,
    all dancing is a chore,
    all music is mere noise.

All the rain of heaven may fall into the sea—
Without love,
    not one drop could become a pearl.

It is said,

   God's Light shines in the six directions.

A shout came from the crowd:

   So where is that Light?
   Shall I fix my gaze to the left,
      or to the right?

It is said,

   For a moment fix it neither to the left
      nor to the right.

If you stay in a king's house
It's because the generous king lets you.
But *you* must make the effort to get there.

Don't be fooled—
The short-cut to the king's house
Is a thousand miles out of the way.

To see the Face of God
      you must move quickly,
      escape every trap,
      and have the strength to keep going.
Yet, in all the eighteen-thousand worlds,
      one with a pure heart
      need not move at all.

People who are sad,
      know not from where that sadness comes.
People who are happy,
      know not from where that happiness comes.
People who search to the left,
      or to the right,
      know not the left from the right.
People who always say, "I and mine,"
      know not what is "I"
      nor what is "mine."

For those in love,
  Moslem, Christian, and Jew do not exist.
For those in love,
  faith and infidelity do not exist.
For those in love,
  body, mind, heart, and soul do not exist.

Why listen to those who see it another way?—
  if they're not in love
  their eyes do not exist.

My scarf, my cape, and my turban—
Someone offered me a nickel for them.

My name, famous throughout the world—
Nobody, Nobody, Nobody—
For a nickel it's yours.

Doing as others told me,
    I was blind.
Coming when others called me,
    I was lost.

Then I left everyone,
    myself as well.
Then I found everyone,
    myself as well.

Don't sit with a sad person,
Only sit with those who are sweet and kind-hearted.
When you've entered a beautiful garden
    Why spend your time with the weeds?
    Stay with the jasmine and the jonquil.

The soul comes once,
    this body a thousand times.

I am everything,
    coming in, going out
    How can I speak of another?

Like a wave my body is here and gone,
Look closely—
    a million waves,
        one sea.

The soul comes once,
    this body a thousand times.

Why talk of the soul? Why mention the body
    when both are myself?

With much effort I have stayed on this path,
    and now this body
    finds a great soul within it.

The soul comes once
    this body a thousand times.

What can I do?—
    I talk yet no one hears me.

I see thousands of people who are myself
Yet they keep thinking they are themselves!

    Love is the morning,
        I, the coming of dawn.
    Love is the rain,
        I, the bloom of Spring.

    Become that love,
        and every burden will be light.
    Become that love
        and every night will shine.

Farewell to myself he is wishing me.
Sitting content he is wishing me.

All my life I tried to please others,
Pleasing myself he is wishing me.

My verses, my poems, my clothes,
   and all I possess;
My virtues, my faults, my pain,
   and my Persian blood—

With the rising tide they come,
With the ebbing waters they go.

Night comes
and the people go to sleep
    like fish returning to water.

When they awake
    some go to work on their jobs,
    some go to work on themselves.

Oh brother, who has ever seen
The morning Sun at midnight?
Who has ever seen a true lover
Mingling with love's pretenders?

You cry out, *Oh, I am burning!*
Cry not—who has ever seen
    A half-baked burning?

If you hurt others, don't expect kindness in return.
One who sows rotten seeds will get rotten fruit.
God is great and compassionate
    but if you plant barley,
        don't expect a harvest of wheat.

They say you bring the word of God
        yet all I hear is talk of good and bad—
        nothing of love or truth.

If someone puts a sign that reads "PRISON"
On the gates of a garden
        What difference does it make?—

        The garden still has flowers,
        The prison still has bars.

O Love,
    they say you are human,
    they say you are divine.
It sounds like you're more famous
    than the Seal of Solomon.

You are the soul
    of every creature
    that crawls the earth—
But my soul knows you in a way
    that only birds can know.

Do you want to be wise?—
    throw all your wisdom away.
Do you want to know love?—
    fill your heart with His love.

Even the water of life
    is jealous of the tears
    that fall from the Lover's eyes.

The moment I heard of His love, I thought,
  To find the Beloved
  I must search with body, mind and soul.

But no—to find the Beloved
  you must become the Beloved.

THE HEART-RAVISHING
BELOVED

Beware! Fly only with the wings of the Shaykh that you may receive the aid of his armies!

One moment the wave of his mercy is your wing; the next moment his painful fire carries you upward.

Do not think that his fire opposes his mercy—behold the unity they share in their effect!

—*Rumi*

The Beloved (or the Master who embodies the Beloved) directs all his actions toward one goal—the annihilation of the disciple's individual self. This "killing" of the ego is what leads him to union with God. Sometimes the Beloved is loving, sometimes He is playful, while at other times He is harsh and ruthless. This ravishing aspect of the Beloved is part of the process of purification called "burning"—a process which is often painful and difficult, but never without great reward. Rumi writes: "It is the burn of the heart that I want. This burn is everything—more precious than a worldly empire—because this is what calls God secretly in the night."

As a chickpea must boil to become edible, as a grape must be stripped of its skin to become wine, as a seed must crack open to become a tree, so the seeker's individuality (which is the sole cause of his pain) must be sacrificed in the fire of love for him to reach perfection. A true seeker understands that this process is necessary and holds to the awareness that the hardship he endures will soon pass, while the treasure he attains will be everlasting.

With your love the fire of youth will rise.
In the heart a vision of the soul will rise.
Go ahead and kill me,
        I know it's what you do—
With your kind of killing, eternal life will rise.

I travelled everywhere,
        following you,
        looking for signs of where you had been—
They show me a house stacked with bodies,
        heads strewn on the floor.

O Beloved, today you want even more:
We're already mad
      and yet you pull
      at the last thread of our sanity.
You've torn away our veil,
You've torn away our clothes.
      We're completely naked!

And still you are tearing!

I want to hold you close,
      like a harp,
      playing the melodies of love.

But you would rather smash open this jar.
      Well, here I am.
      Here are the stones.

When I shed tears of blood,
   You made me laugh.
When I was gone from this world,
   You brought me back.
Now you ask,
   What about your promises?
What promises? —
   You made me break them all.

This Love is the king,
   yet a throne cannot be found.
It is the essence of the Koran
   yet a verse cannot be found.
Any lover hit by the Hunter's arrow
   will bleed all over,
      yet a wound cannot be found.

If only I could be the particles of air
            that surround you
And the dust that falls
            on your feet.

Your pounding seems cruel,
Yet my heart is happy and light—
        Beneath every painful blow
        I feel your tender touch.

We were bound—He added another chain.
We were suffering—He added another grief.
We were lost in a house of mirrors—
        He spun us round and round,
        And added another mirror.

You can't hurt me anymore—
I've become used to your insults
      and your way of killing.

You give me poison—
      it's nectar.
You beat me on the head—
      it's a loving caress.

With this kind of love,
What can I ever reject?

If you get restless, He'll make you wait.
If you fall asleep, He'll wake you up.

If you become a mountain, He'll level you.
If you become the ocean, He'll drink you dry.

I said, *My eyes.*
He said, *They'll flow like the Oxus River.*
I said, *My heart.*
He said, *It will weep all night long.*
I said, *My body.*
He said, *After two or three days I'll ruin it,*
    then dump it outside the city.

I said no more.

I see His face,
I see His smile—
    There is my joy!
I feel His rage
I feel His painful blows—
    There is my joy!

But what's this?—
    He has asked for my head!
At least He has asked me for something—
    There is my joy!

When that Sweetheart saw me all weary and sad,
He came with a smile, stroked my hair,
        and said, *Poor thing,*
        it's really not so good seeing you like this.

He not only put me in this world of fire,
He put a hundred flames on my tongue.

He not only filled the six directions
        with blazing heat—
When I yelled out
        He bound and gagged me!

The smile on your face is sight enough.
The sound of your Name is song enough.
Why cut me down with your deadly arrows
When the shadow of your whip is reason enough?

In the waters of his love I melted like salt—
No good, no bad, no conviction, no doubt remains.

A star has exploded in my heart
And the seven skies are lost in it.

The crucible of His love burns on.
The good ones He throws in,
  the evil ones He spares.

The true lover can't escape this killing.
  The dead man runs for his life!

Do you think I am in control here?
That for a moment, or even half a moment,
  I can tell you what's going on?

I am no more than a pen in a writer's hand,
A ball smacked around by a polo stick.

You ask me about *gold,*
You ask me about *heart*—
O breaker of my heart,
    I know nothing about these!

Where gold? What gold? Whose gold?
    Does a poor man count his gold?!
Where heart? What heart? Whose heart?
    Does a lover speak about his own heart?

Knock,
And He'll open the door.
Vanish,
And He'll make you shine like the Sun.
Fall,
And He'll raise you to the heavens.
Become nothing,
And He'll turn you into everything!

I said, *Tell me what to do.*
　　　He said, *Die.*
I said, *My soul is purer than a mountain stream.*
　　　He said, *Die.*
I said, *But I shine like a candle,*
　　　I'm free like a butterfly. And you,
　　　O your face illumines the whole world . . .
He said, *Die.*

Being away from you,
　　　I have become used to these tears.

I am a candle, melting with grief,
A heart, alive
　　　by the sound of its own weeping.

Dearly I hold
This longing in my heart,
For I know it is only found
    in sacred places.

This longing,
too large for heaven and earth,
fits easily in my heart,
    smaller than the eye of a needle.

Within my sadness is joy.
Lying on the ground
    I can touch the heavens.

Silent like the earth
    my cries can be heard
    beyond the turning of the Great Wheel.

Oh I'm alive,
But this pain is worse than death.
My heart pounds, my body shakes,
    my stomach burns with pangs of hunger.
At least with hunger
    the more you eat, the better it gets,
But not with this,
    for the more I eat, the worse it gets.

All this longing
Has made me red in the face.
I have become beastly,
Crippled, angry, and a worthless being—
        No, no—
    I am a lover of love.
    I am a mighty lion
    Thinking I am a lamb.

I say, *My eyes.* You say, *Look for Him.*
I say, *My gut.* You say, *Tear it open.*

I say, *My heart.* You ask, *What's inside?*
I say *My longing.* You say, *That's all you need.*

I have no idea where to go
        or what to do!
Sitting by your side gives me no comfort,
        living without you is impossible.
I am lost in a hopeless dilemma—
No, this is not a dilemma,
        there is no way out of this pain.

Enough, enough, enough with this burning!
We turn our backs on that Lover
    who never visits us anyway.
We turn away from Mecca.
We turn away from the holy books.
We even throw the saints out of the city.

So . . . When are you coming?

I cried, and I burned in that cry.
I kept silent, and I burned in that silence.
Then I stayed away from extremes—
    I went right down the middle—
And I burned in that middle.

I am dead to this world.
      I've been this way a long time.
Every day my body grows weaker
      and one day it will fall back into the earth.
It's not difficult to renounce this life
      and this world,
But to give up your love,
      that is difficult—
      no, impossible.

      Love came and it made me empty.
Love came and it filled me with the Beloved.
      It became the blood in my body,
      It became my arms and my legs.
      It became everything!
Now all I have is a name,
      the rest belongs to the Beloved.

UNION
(THE WEDDING NIGHT)

The complete and final merging of the individual soul (lover) with God (the Beloved) is known to the Sufis as "the Wedding Night." This marks the ultimate attainment, the endless ecstasy, the drop once again becoming the sea.

Union with the Beloved is the goal of all Sufi practice. This union brings the startling realization that one's own soul *is* the Beloved, that one's own soul *is* the very thing he's been searching for. A great master once said, "All of creation sings the song of union with the Beloved. Every action of every soul, whether he knows it or not, is seeking one thing—union with the Beloved."

Tonight we go to that place of eternity.
This is the wedding night—
        a never-ending union
        of lover and Beloved.

We whisper gentle secrets to each other
        and the child of the universe
        takes its first breath.

So you want to put your neck
        in the shackles of love?
Well then, don't complain about the pain
        and the hardships.
Just go through them with a quiet mind.

        In the end your rusty chains
        Will become a necklace of gold.

Now that you are free of this world
What makes you think
    you can stay separate from it?
Did you not know?—
    The moment you became the moon,
    You became the most visible light in the sky.

My heart is cleansed by His sweet water;
Now my love blossoms without a thorn.
I hear that love
    is the key to every heart.
But if there is no lock,
    why talk about keys?

So you want union?

Union is not something found on the ground
     or purchased at the marketplace.
Union comes only at the cost of life.
Otherwise, everyone and his brother
     would have this union.

With every step I take
     another attachment falls away.

I take a hundred steps,
the veils fall,
The Beloved appears—
     beautiful, radiant—
I am in love!

O brother, can't you see?—
It is myself I have fallen in love with!

O Love,
When I search for you
  I find you searching for me.
When I look around
  I find the locks of your hair
  in my own hands.

I always thought I was drunk on your wine,
But now I find your wine is drunk on me.

I am the mirror and the face in it.
I am the song and the one who sings it.
I am illness and its cure.
I am the sweet water
  and the glass filled to the brim.

Without looking
I can see everything within myself.

Why should I bother my eyes anymore
Now that I see the whole world with His eyes?

Some day our souls will be one
And our union will be forever.

I know that everything I give you
    comes back to me.
So I give you my life,
    hoping that *you*
    will come back to me.

You ask for profit—
        don't run from your customers.
You ask for the moon—
        don't run from the night.
You ask for a rose—
        don't run from the thorns.
You ask for the Beloved—
        don't run from yourself.

Do not look for God,
Look for the one
        looking for God.
But why look at all?—
        He is not lost,
        He is right here,

Closer than your own breath.

The marvelous sound
That comes from the sky—I am That.
The sweet fragrance
That comes from the garden—I am That.

The great beauty
That comes from the heart and soul
Until I leave . . . Wait!
I can't leave—I am That.

I am filled with splendor,
        spinning with your love.

It looks like I'm spinning around you,
        but no—I'm spinning around myself!

This silence is worth
More than a thousand lives,
This freedom worth
More than all the empires on earth.

To glimpse that truth within yourself,
For even just a moment, is worth
More than all heavens, all worlds,
All this, and all that.

You call him a moon,
        yet moonlight fades.
You call him a king,
        yet kingdoms fall.

How often you say,
        Wake up, you'll miss the sunrise.
But His Sun always shines within me.
How can I miss the sunrise?

By day I praised you
And never knew it.
By night I stayed with you
And never knew it.

I always thought that I was me—but no,
I was you
And never knew it!

A step toward your own heart
    is a step toward the Beloved.

In this house of mirrors
    you see a lot of things—
Rub your eyes,
Only you exist.

There is a force within
Which gives you life—
        seek That.
In your body
Lies a priceless gem—
        seek That.
O wandering Sufi,
        if you want to find
        the greatest treasure
        Don't look outside,
Look inside, and seek That.

All my talk was madness,
        filled with *do*s and *don't*s.

For ages I knocked on a door—
        when it opened I found
        I was knocking from the inside!

ODES

ALCHEMIST OF MY SOUL

O limitless and compassionate one,
high above the rest,
You have set ablaze the dry weeds of intellect.
You have come with a smile,
and thrown open the gates of my prison.
You have come to the lowly
and given to them with the generosity of God.

You are the call of the rising Sun,
the hope of all people in need.
You are the seeker, the goal,
and seeking itself.
Blazing like fire in every heart,
    calming the mind of its restlessness,
you are the seer, the seen, and sight itself.

O Alchemist of my soul, essence of all truth,
once your cure appeared
everything else lost its meaning.

There was a time we lost ourselves in others,
a time we ate the best of foods.
There was a time we relied on the intellect,
a time we looked for fortune—
    but all this had no value in the end.

For a mouthful of food and some bitter herbs
we went everywhere,
we made so many plans—
    one day it was Rome,
    the next day it was Africa.

We entered a raging battlefield, for what?—
a few crumbs of bread.

Lose your soul in God's love, I swear
there is no other way.

Stay with that silence.
I once ran toward the knowledge of this world;
now the papers are packed, the pens are broken—
O *Saaqi,* bring on the wine!

O MASTER, COME HERE!

O master, come here!
O master, come here!

O lost lover,
        enchanted by the universe, come here!
O heart ever-thirsty,
O righteous king, come here!

You are the feet, you are the hands,
        you are the life of all that lives;
Drunken flight of the nightingale,
        toward this garden—come here!

You are the ears, the eyes,
        and the senses beyond.
You are the wanderer without food—
        To this banquet, come here!

You are hidden from view,
        and all that is seen
Dancing carefree—
        come here!

You are the light of day,
        the joy of love,
        the searing pain of sorrow.
O night-glow of the moon,
Cloud of sweet dew, come here!

O wisdom of all worlds,
        knower of all knowledge,

At times you are here,
At times you are gone;
Now rise up and stay forever.

O blood-stained heart
        your jubilee and madness are over—
        the grapes have turned to wine.
Please, no more tears, just come here!

O sleepless nights, begone.
O needless sorrow, begone.
O tired intellect, begone.
To that awakened land, come here!

O weary heart, come here,
O wounded soul, come here;
And if the doorway is blocked,
Through the wall, come here!

O beauty of Noah, come here,
O longing of the soul, come here,
O cure for the weary, come here,
O medicine for the sick, come here.

O face of shining moonlight, come here,
O waters of the heart, come here,
O happiness of lovers, come here,
O blindness of fools, come here.

O voice of the soul . . .
Enough! The tongue is getting tired.

Without another breath,
Without another word, come!

DON'T LEAVE ME UNBAKED

Be a lover for me, a cave for me,
The sweet burn of love for me.
O master, protect me!

You are Noah, you are the soul,
        you are the slayer and the slain.
You are the treasure of knowledge—
O master, open your secret door for me!

You are the light and the celebration;
        the land rejoicing in victory.
You are the great bird of Mount Sinai—
O master, don't drop me from your beak!

You are the ocean, and the shore;
        a kind word, and a heart
        filled with despair.
You are the sugar and the poison—
O master, more sugar and less poison!

You are the orb of the Sun,
        and the house of Venus,
You are the light of hope
        that touches the world.
O master, open up and let me see you!

You are the pain of hunger
        and the crumbs of every beggar.
You are the water overflowing.
O master, fill my empty cup!

You are the bait and the trap,
    the wine and the glass.
You are the heat
    and the bread in the oven.
O master, don't leave me unbaked!

This body is not fast enough
    to reach the end
    of Love's path.
Let me enter that emptiness—
O master, take away all these words of mine.

CAN'T YOU SEE THE MIGHTY WARRIOR?

How often you ask,
> *What is my path?*
> *What is my cure?*—
He has made you a seeker of Unity,
    isn't that enough?

All your sorrow exists for one reason—
    that you may end sorrow forever.
The desire to know your own soul
    will end all other desires.

The smell of bread has reached you—
    if that aroma fills you with delight
    what need is there for bread?
If you have fallen in love,
    that love is proof enough;
If you have not fallen in love,
    what good is all your proof?

Can't you see?—
If you are not the King
    what meaning is there
    in a kingly entourage?
If the beautiful one is not inside you
    what is that light
    hidden under your cloak?

From a distance you tremble with fear—

Can't you see the mighty warrior
    standing ready in your heart?

The fire of his eyes
    has burned away every veil,
So why do you remain behind the curtain,
    scared of what you cannot see?—
Open your eyes! The Beloved
    is staring you right in the face!

If a master has not placed
His light in your heart,
What joy can you find in this world?—

    every flower is lifeless,
    and sweet wine has no taste.

ONE WHISPER OF THE BELOVED

Lovers share a sacred decree—
     to seek the Beloved.
They roll head over heels,
     rushing toward the Beautiful One
     like a torrent of water.

In truth, everyone is a shadow of the Beloved—
     Our seeking is *His* seeking,
     Our words are *His* words.

At times we flow toward the Beloved
     like a dancing stream.
At times we are still water
     held in His pitcher.
At times we boil in a pot
     turning to vapor—
     that is the job of the Beloved.

He breathes into my ear
     until my soul
     takes on His fragrance.
He is the soul of my soul—
     How can I escape?
But why would any soul in this world
     want to escape from the Beloved?

He will melt your pride
     making you thin as a strand of hair,
Yet do not trade, even for both worlds,
One strand of His hair.

We search for Him here and there
        while looking right at Him.
Sitting by His side we ask,
"O Beloved, where is the Beloved?"

Enough with such questions!—
Let silence take you to the core of life.

All your talk is worthless
When compared to one whisper
        of the Beloved.

THE STILL-POINT OF ECSTASY

On the Night of Creation I was awake,
Busy at work while everyone slept.
I was there to see the first wink
    and hear the first tale told.
I was the first one caught
    in the hair of the Great Imposter.

Whirling around the still-point of ecstasy
I spun like the wheel of heaven.

    How can I describe this to you?—
        you were born later.

I was a companion of that Ancient Lover;
Like a bowl with a broken rim
    I endured his tyranny.
Why shouldn't I be as lustrous as the King's cup?—
    I have lived in the room of treasures.
Why shouldn't this bubble become the sea?—
    I am the secret that lies at its bottom . . .

Sh . . . no more words—
Hear only the voice within.
Remember, the first thing He said was:
    We are beyond words.

WHAT A BLESSING

Don't hide—the sight of your face is a blessing.
Wherever you place your foot,
    there rests a blessing.
Even your shadow,
    passing over me like a swift bird,
    is a blessing.

The great Spring has come.
Your sweet air,
    blowing through the city, the country,
    the gardens, and the desert
    is a blessing.

He has come with love to our door;
    His knock is a blessing.

We go from house to house, asking of him.
    Any answer is a blessing.

Caught in this body,
    we look for a sight of the soul.
Remember what the Prophet said:
    One sight is a blessing.

The leaf of every tree brings a message
    from the Unseen world.
Look! Every falling leaf is a blessing.

All of Nature swings in unison—
    singing without tongues,

listening without ears.
What a blessing!

O soul, the four elements are your face—
Water, wind, fire, and earth—
    Each one is a blessing.

Once the seed of faith takes root
    it cannot be blown away,
    even by the strongest wind—
    Now that's a blessing!

I bow to you,
    for the dust of your feet
    is the crown on my head.
As I walk toward you,
    every step I take is a blessing.

    His form appeared before me, just now,
        as I was singing this poem. I swear.
    What a blessing!
    What a blessing!

Every vision born of earth is fleeting;
Every vision born of heaven is a blessing.

For people, the sight of Spring warms their hearts;
For fish, the rhythm of the ocean
    is a blessing.
The brilliant Sun
    that shines in every heart—
    for the heavens, earth, and all creatures—
    What a blessing!

The heart can't wait to speak of this ecstasy.
The soul is kissing the earth saying,
O God, what a blessing!

Fill me with the wine of your silence.
Let it soak my every pore
For the inner splendor it reveals
    is a blessing,
    is a blessing.

THIS IS MY WISH

O harp,
>   the strains of a longing heart is my wish.
O flute,
>   your burning cry is my wish.

Play the great song of Arabia;
I am the Great Bird,
>   and the song of Solomon is my wish.

Play the song of Iraq,
>   and let its soothing melody
>   calm the hearts of its people—
>   this is my wish.

Play on! Play on!—
High notes, low notes, every note.

I have fallen into a dream
>   with your peaceful melody.
Now awaken me with a loud gong—
>   this is my wish.

I hear your song—
>   the voice of God,
>   a symphony of love playing to the world.
That music is my witness—
I am a pious man,
>   pure faith is my wish.

O love, vanquish the intellect;
O love, that bewildering moment
    is my wish.

O sweet wind,
passing over love's grass,
    blow in my direction,
      for the fragrance of love is my wish.

In the Face of my master, all beauty is revealed.

One sight—
One sight—
      that is my wish.

STILL SOME SECRETS

O friend, can't you see?—
Your face is glowing with light.
  The whole world could get drunk
  on the love found in *your* heart.

Don't run here and there
  looking all around—
He is right inside you.

Is there any place where the Sun doesn't shine?
Is there anyone who can't see the full Moon?

    Veil upon veil, thought upon thought—
    Let go of them all,
    For they only hide the truth.

Once you see the glory
Of his moon-like face,
  what excuse could you have
  for pain or sorrow?

Any heart without his love—
even the king's heart—
  is a coffin for the dead.

Everyone can see God
  within his own heart—
  everyone who is not a corpse.
Everyone can drink
  from the waters of life
  and conquer death forever.

The veil of ignorance
    covers the Sun and Moon;
It even causes Love to think, *I am not divine.*

O Shams, Blazing Light of Tabriz,
There are still some secrets of yours
that even I cannot tell.

YOU CAME TO SEE THE
SUN RISE

O friend,
You came to see the Sun rise,
But instead you see us,
Whirling like a confusion of atoms—
    Who could be so lucky?

Who comes to a lake for water
And sees the reflection of the moon?

Who, blind like Jacob,
Seeks his lost son,
And regains the light of his own eyes?

Who, parched with thirst,
Lowers a bucket into a well
And comes up with an ocean of nectar?
    Who could be so lucky?

Who, like Moses, approaches a desert bush
And beholds the fire
    of a hundred dawns?

Who, like Jesus, enters a house to avoid capture,
And discovers a passage to the other world?

Who, like Solomon, cuts open the stomach of a fish
And finds a golden ring?
    Who could be so lucky?

An assassin rushes in to kill the Prophet,
And stumbles upon a fortune.

An oyster, opens his mouth for a drop of water,
And discovers a shining pearl within himself.

A poor man, searches through a heap of garbage
And finds a magnificent treasure—
    Who could be so lucky?

O friend,
Forget all your stories and fancy words.
Let friend and stranger look upon you
And see a flood of light!—
The door of heaven opening!
    Let them be so lucky!

And what of those
Who walk toward Shamsuddin?
Their feet grow weary,
Their backs grow weak,
They fall to the ground in utter exhaustion.
But then come the wings of His love,
Lifting them,
          upward.

    Who could be so lucky?

A BREAKING WAVE OF LOVE

Ah, once more he put a fire in me,
And once more this crazy heart
    is craving the open plains.
This ocean of love breaks into another wave
And blood pours from my heart
    in all directions.

Ah, one spark flew
    and burned the house of my heart.
Smoke filled the sky.
The flames grew fierce in the wind.

The fire of the heart is not easily lit.
So don't cry out: "O Lord, rescue me
    from the burning flames!
Spare me from the army of thoughts
    that is marching through my mind!"

O Heart of Pure Consciousness,
You are the ruler of all hearts.
After countless ages
    you brought my soul
    all it ever wished for.

The eyes of all people happy and sad,
    are closed to the truth.
May their eyes be opened!
May they look upon God
    and get drunk on His beauty.

May their hands reach toward the Truth.
May their ears hear the voice of the Beloved.
May the shadow of a Master
     fall upon everyone who has devotion.

All the world praises you,
But where did this "you" come from?
All the universe is born of Love—
But where did this Love come from?

O Shams,
     you are the owner of the land of life—
     the light of every heart;
Even the King of Love
     knows no love
     that is not yours.

THE MANY OBJECTS OF DESIRE

Oh, the many objects of desire,
The many reflections of His beautiful Face.
How can you turn away from such eyes?
Where, where will you turn?

A thousand praises!
A thousand hearts of gratitude!
For your love has given wings to the world.
Wanting to see the dawn of your eternal light,
This old world recites your Name each morning.
You have shared your love;
You have ruled with kindness.
How can there be justice
        without your purity and compassion?

I heard that Joseph did not sleep for ten years;
The prince of virtue kept praying to God
        for the sake of his brothers:

> *O God, forgive them—*
>   *if not, I'll cry a hundred tears.*
> *Do not punish them*
>   *for they truly regret the evil act*
>   *they so suddenly committed.*

Joseph's feet swelled from standing all night:
His eyes burned from tears and torment.
His cries echoed through the heavens
        and rocked the flight of angels;
It caused the Sea of Compassion to boil
        and overflow its bounds . . .

Such is the way of spiritual masters—
     they work day and night to release mankind
     from its pain and moral decay.

After helping one soul, they move on,
     and God alone knows
     of their great compassion.
Like water seeking low ground,
Masters always ask God
     to rescue those who are lost.
They take away despair,
     and replace it with joy;
They remove the tattered clothes of life
     and dress everyone in silk.

Enough for now!
I'll tell you the rest tomorrow . . .
Now look how the beauty of the moon
Shows only through a dark night.

O WHISPERING BREEZE

O whispering breeze,
    bring the news of my beloved Shams.
It would be worth more
    than all the amber and musk
    from China to Constantinople.

Please tell me if you've heard a word
    from his sweet lips,
    or a beat of his pounding heart.

O, just one word from Shams,
    and I'd gladly give my life.

His love is before me and behind me;
Through his love
    my heart has become pure,
    my breast has imbibed every virtue.

One smell of his perfume
    and I walk light-headed on this path.
O *Saaqi,* enough with your wine—
    I am drunk on the wine from his cup!
My nose is so full of his fragrance
    that I have no need for incense, musk,
    or the fine amber of Mongolia.

Shamsuddin is forever alive in my heart.
Shamsuddin is the generosity of every soul.
Shamsuddin is poverty,
Shamsuddin is the purest of all wealth.

I am not the only one

singing, *Shamsuddin, Shamsuddin*—
The nightingales sing from the garden,
And the partridge from the mountainside.

The beauty of a starry night is Shamsuddin.
The Garden of Paradise is Shamsuddin.
Love, compassion, and gratitude are Shamsuddin.

Shamsuddin is the brightness of day,
Shamsuddin is the turning sky,
Shamsuddin is time everlasting,
Shamsuddin is the endless treasure.

Shamsuddin is the King of Cups,
Shamsuddin is the ocean of nectar.
Shamsuddin is the breath of Jesus,
Shamsuddin is the face of Joseph.

O God, show me that inner place,
    where we can sit together,
Shams in the middle, my soul by his side.

Shamsuddin is sweeter than life,
Shamsuddin is an earth full of sugar,
Shamsuddin is the towering cypress,
Shamsuddin is the flowering Spring.

Shamsuddin is the well of clear water,
Shamsuddin is the harp and rubaab,
Shamsuddin is the barrel of wine,
Shamsuddin is the bliss of my soul.

O Shams, you are the hope of every heart,
    the one every lover longs to hear.
O Shams, come back, alas,
Don't leave my soul in ruins.

THE SHINING HERO

Every prisoner, I freed.
Every lover's soul, I made happy.
    The mouth of the dragon—I tore it open.
    The path of love—I made it smooth.

Out of water I weaved the world.
Then I filled it with the power of life.
Out of water I brought forth living images
    that cannot be carved from ivory or box wood.

Water bursts forth, surging
    with the ecstasy of creation—
That is its nature,
That is its addiction.

I pulled Joseph out of a well,
And summoned the whole world
    to remember his name.

I am the King
    who enjoys the sight of every Queen.
I am the shining hero
    who cut through a mountain of stone
    for the sake of love

I have caused great gardens to bloom;
I have built great empires.
The universe is my witness—
I am a King who gives away land
    and rules with perfect justice.
The earth is my witness—

I am merely a guest, born in this world
        to know the secrets
        that lie beyond it.

What masters I have checkmated!
What novices I have turned to masters!

Many lions have roared at me,
Yet like a fox,
I tamed them and made them helpless.

Enough with your doubts!
Enough with your sorrows!
Let them all go,
        and I will show you the way.

Everyone swept up by the storm of misery
Will be brought to solid ground—
        all they must do is call out to me.
I'll bring them from the center of the whirlwind
Just as I brought this whole creation
        out of Emptiness . . .

Now my master has bade me to keep silent—
He has struck me with his sword
        and turned my tongue to steel.
        Now all I can do is cut.

THE STAFF OF MOSES

I am in your garden
    beneath a tree that grants every wish.
I am so full of fire
    that I dance without music.

I am a shadow
    forever dancing with the sunlight—
At times I lie on the ground,
At times I stand on my head.
    At times I am short,
    At times I am long.

Like the movement of dark and light
    across the earth,
    I move across the ages.
I am the Ruler of the Egyptians
    and the Guide of the Jews.
Among men of letters
I am the law of truth—
At times I am like a pen,
At times like the staff of Moses,
At times like a cobra
    slithering its way through the sand.

Don't try to find love
By leaning on the cane of the intellect;
    that cane is nothing
    but a blind man's stick.
One sign from you is all I want;

One "yes" from you
    and my soul will be free.

I am not from this place.
I am a stranger here,
Walking blindly,
Hoping you will come and show me
    where to take my next step.

THIS WILL NOT WIN HIM

Reason says,
>   I will win him with my eloquence.

Love says,
>   I will win him with my silence.

Soul says,
>   How can I ever win him
>   When all I have is already his?

He does not want, he does not worry,
He does not seek a sublime state of euphoria—
>   How then can I win him
>   With sweet wine or gold? . . .

He is not bound by the senses—
>   How then can I win him
>   With all the riches of China?

He is an angel,
Though he appears in the form of a man.
Even angels cannot fly in his presence—
>   How then can I win him
>   By assuming a heavenly form?

He flies on the wings of God,
His food is pure light—
>   How then can I win him
>   With a loaf of baked bread?

He is neither a merchant, nor a tradesman—
    How then can I win him
    With a plan of great profit?

He is not blind, nor easily fooled—
    How then can I win him
    By lying in bed as if gravely ill?

I will go mad, pull out my hair,
Grind my face in the dirt—
    How will this win him?

    He sees everything—
    how can I ever fool him?

He is not a seeker of fame,
A prince addicted to the praise of poets—
    How then can I win him
    With flowing rhymes and poetic verses?

The glory of his unseen form
Fills the whole universe,
    How then can I win him
    With a mere promise of paradise?

I may cover the earth with roses,
I may fill the ocean with tears,
I may shake the heavens with praises—
    none of this will win him.

There is only one way to win him,
    this Beloved of mine—

Become his.

THE ARROWS OF LARGER BOWS

I am a lover,
    and from His love
    I did not escape.
I am a warrior,
    and from the field of battle
    I did not escape.

Like a lion, I attacked lions,
but in the middle, like a fox,
    I did not escape.

Though my aim was the cupola of heaven,
from the snares of this world,
    I did not escape.

I was the medicine for every illness,
but from the pain of others
    I did not escape.

I revered the prophets with all my soul,
but from evil company
    I did not escape.

    I am alive in this little box called life;
    I am alive because my soul
      did not escape.

The only reason I get hit
by the arrows of his eyes
is because from the arrows of larger bows
    I did not escape.

The wounds of battle have turned to victory
because of the pain
    I did not escape.

I am floating in a sea of nectar,
filled with every delight,
because of the hardships
    I did not escape.

When my Master showed himself to me
I was stunned, I could not move—
From the onrush of both worlds
    I could not escape!

THE BODY IS TOO SLOW FOR ME

Toward the gardens,
Toward the orchards,
    I am going.
If you want to stay here,
Stay here—
    I am going!
My day is dark without His Face,
Toward that bright flame
    I am going.

My soul is racing ahead of me.
It says, *The body is too slow for me*—
    I am going.

The smell of apples arises
    from the orchard of my soul.
One whiff and I am gone—
    Toward a feast of apples
    I am going.

A sudden wind won't blow me over.
Toward Him, like a mountain of iron,
    I am going.

My shirt is ripped open
    with the pain of loss.
Searching for a new life,
    with my head held high,
    I am going.

I am fire, though I seem like oil—
   Seeking to be the fuel of *His* fire,
   I am going.

I appear as a steady mountain
Yet bit by bit,
Toward that tiny opening
   I am going.

THIS IS LOVE

This is love—to fly upward
    toward the endless heavens.
To rend a hundred veils at every moment.
At the first breath, to give up life;
At the final step, to go without feet.
To see the world as a dream
    and not as it appears.

I said, O heart
What a blessing it is
To join the circle of lovers,
    To see beyond sight,
    To know the secrets within every breast.

I said, O soul
From where comes your life
And the power of your spirit?
    Tell me, speak in the language of birds,
    And I will understand.

My soul said to me:
They brought me to God's workshop
Where all things take form—and I flew.
    Before this form of mine
    was even shaped—I flew and I flew.

And when I could fly no longer
They dragged me into this form,
    and locked me into this house
    of water and clay.

THE MAN OF GOD

The man of God
Is drunk, but drinks no wine;
He is full, but eats no meat.

The man of God
Spins with ecstasy,
And doesn't care about food or sleep;
He is a king beneath a simple cloak,
A diamond amidst the falling ruins.

The man of God
Is not of air, nor earth;
Not of fire, nor water.
He is the pearl of a shoreless sea,
A cloudless sky dripping with nectar.
He is a boundless heaven,
With a hundred moons
And a hundred suns shining.

His wisdom
Is born of the supreme truth,
Not from the pages of a book.
He is beyond faith and doubt,
He knows not right nor wrong.

The man of God
Has bid farewell to Nothingness
And has returned in all his glory.

The man of God is well-hidden.
O my soul, Go! Find him in your heart!

FROM BOX TO BOX

D on't weep.
The joy that has gone
    will come 'round again in another form—
Have no doubt about this!

A child's first joy
    comes from its mother's milk;
After the child is weaned
    his joy comes from drinking sweet wine.

This supreme joy has no resting place—
It enters one form then another,
    from box to box—an eternal movement
    between heaven and earth.

Here it comes, pouring down from the sky,
    seeping into the earth,
    and rising up again as a bed of roses.

Now it is water, now a plate of rice,
Now the swaying trees, now a horse and rider.
It lies within these forms for awhile
    then bursts forth to become something new.

Isn't this like our dreams?—
The body sleeps
    while the soul moves on
    to take other forms.
You say,
    I dreamt I was a cypress, a bed of tulips,
    the blossoms of roses and jasmines.

Then the soul returns, and you wake up—
       the cypress is gone, the roses are gone.

I tell you truly,
       everything you now see
       will vanish like a dream.

I do not mean to trouble you, O friend,
       with words so bold as these.
Perhaps you will only listen to God.
       He speaks more gently than I.

But how will you ever hear Him with
All that blathering going on?—
       Everyone is speaking about golden bread
       yet no one has ever tasted it!

O my soul, where can I find rest
       but in the shimmering love of his heart?
Where can I see the pure light of the Sun
       but in the eyes of my own Shams-e Tabriz?

THE SWEETEST OF ALL THINGS

Since you are the one who takes life
It is the sweetest of all things to die.
Life is sweet
But merging with you is far sweeter.

Come into the garden!
Join the Friend of the Truth!
In his garden you'll drink the Water of Life,
    though it seems like fire to die.

In one moment someone dies,
In the next moment someone is born.
There is a lot of coming and going
    no one really dies
    nor will I ever die.

Forget the body, become pure spirit.
Dance from here to the other world.
Don't stop. Don't try to escape,
    even if you are afraid to die.

I swear were it not for His pure nature
The wheel of heaven would turn to dust.
Merge with Him now,
And you'll be sweeter than halva
    when it comes time to die.

Why hold on to this life?—
True living comes by giving up this life.
Why cling to one piece of gold?—
    it is a mine of gold to die.

Escape from this cage
and breathe the scented air of His garden.
Break this hard shell—
        It's like a shining pearl to die.

When God calls and pulls you close,
Going is like paradise—
It's like a heavenly river to die.

Death is only a mirror
And your true nature is reflected there.
See what the mirror is saying—
        it's quite a sight to die!

If you are kind and faithful
Your death will also be that way.
If you are cruel and faithless,
        that is the way you will die.

If you are like Joseph,
        full of goodness,
That's how your mirror will be.
If not, you will see
        only fear and torment
        when it comes time to die.

These words are sweet,
        but they always fade.
Sh . . . The eternal Khezr
        and the Water of Life
        have no idea what it means to die.

BECOME THE BELOVED

Let go of your fancy illusions;
O lovers, become mad, become mad.
Rise up from life's raging fire,
        become a bird, become a bird.

Lose yourself completely,
Turn your house into ruins,
Then join the lovers of God—
        become a Sufi, become a Sufi.

Cleanse your heart of its old regrets,
Wash it seven times;
Then let the wine of love be poured—
        become a cup, become a cup.

Fill your soul with so much love
        that it becomes the Supreme Soul.
Run toward the saints,
        become drunk, become drunk.

That King who hears everything
        is conversing with a pious man.
To hear those sacred words
        become pure, become pure.

Your spirit was lifted to the heavens
        when you heard my sweet song.
Now your limits are gone.
Like a fearless lover
        become a legend, become a legend.

Turn a night of sleep
        into a night of divine revelation!
Hold the grace of God—
        become His home, become His home.

Your thoughts will take you
        wherever they please—
        don't follow them!
Follow your destiny
        and become the Self, become the Self.

Passion and desire bind your heart.
Remove the locks—
        become a key, become a key . . .

Solomon speaks with the language of the birds—
Listen! Don't be the trap
        that falcons flee—
        become a nest, become a nest.

If the Sweetheart reveals Her beauty,
        become a mirror.
If She lets down Her hair,
        become a comb, become a comb.

How long will you be two-faced?
How long will you lack self-will
        and flap in the wind like a flag?
How long will you be like a chess bishop
        moving only diagonally—
        become a Sage, become a Sage.

Out of gratitude you gave away
        some possessions and some vanity.

Now give away everything—
    become gratitude itself, become gratitude itself.

For a time you were the elements,
For a time you were an animal,
For a time you will be a soul—
    Now is your chance—
Become the Supreme Soul, become the Supreme Soul.

O preacher,
How long will you yell from the rooftops
    and knock on the doors of others?—
Look inside your own home.
You've talked about love long enough—
    now become the Beloved, become the Beloved!

DOORS IN METAL

Tell me, O Love,
Who is more elegant,
You or this vast garden of yours?

Shine, O moon,
You are an inspiration
to all who look upon the night sky.

Sour will turn to sweet,
Blasphemy will turn to truth,
Thorn bushes will turn to jonquil,
A hundred bodies will spring to life
        with one breath of yours.

You place doors in the sky.
You place wings on the human heart.
You enchant every mind
        and bewilder both worlds.

        O Beloved,
        your face is sweet and rosy red,
        how rosy red.

        O Beloved,
        yours is the pleasure of this world
        and the way to the next.

The threshed corn assumes your color;
All truth becomes one
        under the stamping of your foot.
Every note of my song

longs to ring
with the sweetness of your voice.

Without you, the markets would be empty,
The gardens and the vineyards
would wash away in the rain.

You show trees how to sway in the wind.
You show wet branches how to weep.

The leaves and fruits get drunk
on your life-giving water.
If the vast gardens wished for one thing
During the eternal Spring
it would be for leaves, flying forever,
in this flower-wind of yours.

The lights of heaven and the moving planets
Think little of any star
that dares to shine
in this vast galaxy of yours.

O, what a promise you have made!
To serve joy instead of bread
to any soul who becomes a guest of yours. . . .
I went somewhere and I returned.
In a moment, as in a dream,
I was at the beginning and the end;
This elephant of a soul
saw the open plains of yours.

From all my plans I gained nothing.
In the end my heart broke its chains,

        grabbed my soul,
        and dragged it into your presence.
There I see no pettiness, no pain.
Every moment a new life enters,
        born from the flowing compassion of yours.

O, the mountain looks small
        beside your grandeur
And the heart seems rude
        beside your love . . .

You are holding every door wide open.
Doors in metal, in mountains, in stone!
Yet my heart crawls around like an ant
        looking for its tiny hole.

I may sing till the end of time
Trying to describe your face
        but I'll always sound mute.
How can a person talk straight
        when he is in love?
How can a person walk straight
        when he is drowning
        in this wine-filled ocean of yours?

THE RHYTHM OF OUR HEARTS

The Light of your Face
    illumines the universe;
And from that Light, in all ages,
    you have taken form.

You are the *Saaqi*
    and the wine of victory—
That is what you will always be.
Can blown glass return to the fire?
Can aged wine turn back into grapes?

You shape the destiny of every soul,
    renewing this weary world.
Every night you bring another joy,
    every night a celebration.

Love and ecstasy is our calling now—
O Beloved, you will dance forever
    as the rhythm of our hearts.

YOU AND I

Happy is the moment, when we sit together,
With two forms, two faces, yet one soul,
     you and I.

The flowers will bloom forever,
The birds will sing their eternal song,
The moment we enter the garden,
     you and I.

The stars of heaven will come out to watch us,
And we will show them
     the light of a full moon—
     you and I.

No more thought of "you" and "I."
Just the bliss of union—
Joyous, alive, free of care, you and I.

All the bright-winged birds of heaven
Will swoop down to drink of our sweet water—
The tears of our laughter, you and I.

What a miracle of fate, us sitting here.
Even at the opposite ends of the earth
We would still be together, you and I.

We have one form in this world,
     another in the next.
To us belongs an eternal heaven,
     the endless delight of you and I.

TWO HUNDRED JUPITERS
ARE DRUNK ON MY MOON

Two hundred Jupiters are drunk on my Moon.
One blink of his eyes has enchanted
    a hundred Samaritans.
His every word blazes with the call, *I am the way,*
lighting a fire in the belly of every infidel.

The burning flame of his heart
has reached the heavens
and his life-giving spirit has turned the horizon red. . . .

    O Lion of God, to where are you rushing?
    O Great Solomon, your Seal is the crown
    of all angels and demons.

    O Nimble Soul,
    you are moving so fast
    that you don't even care to look
    at the ones you have just slaughtered.
    You hear the screams of the killing-ground
    but do not even break your stride to listen!

He looked at me with his dagger-gaze.
I drowned in the waters of his eyes.
Through the scalding pain of non-existence
I am gone, vanished. I have become
    Shamsuddin, the Light of Tabriz.

Now I will let *Shams* tell my story,
    for all my words are his.

EVERY SWEET SONG OF MINE

You are my Sultan, you are my Lord;
You are my heart, my soul, and the faith of mine.

By your breath I am alive;
What is one life?—you are a hundred lives of mine.

Without you, bread cannot feed a man;
You are the water and the bread of mine.

By your touch, poison becomes medicine;
You are the cure and sweet nectar of mine.

You are the garden, the grass, and the heavens;
You are the cypress, and the laughing jasmine of mine.

I have entered that supreme silence.
Please, you go on. . . .
My mouth may open, words may come out,
But you are every sweet song of mine.

A WORLD INSIDE THIS WORLD

There is another world inside this one—
    no words can describe it.
There is living, but no fear of death;
There is Spring, but never a turn to Autumn.
There are legends and stories
    coming from the walls and ceilings.
Even the rocks and trees recite poetry.

Here an owl becomes a peacock,
A wolf becomes a beautiful shepherd.
To change the scenery, change your mood;
To move around, just will it.

Stand for a moment
And look at a desert of thorns—
    it becomes a flowery garden.
See that boulder on the ground?
It moves, and a mine of rubies appears.
    Wash your hands and face
    in the waters of this place—
The cooks have prepared a great feast!

Here all beings give birth to angels.
When they see me ascending to the heavens
    every corpse springs back to life.

I have seen many kinds of trees
    growing from the Earth,
But who has ever seen the birth of paradise?

I have seen water, but who has ever seen
    one drop of water
    give birth to a hundred warriors?

Who could ever imagine such a place?
    Such a heaven? Such a Garden of Eden?

Whoever reads this poem—translate it.
    Tell the whole world about this place!

WHO AM I?

What is to be done, O brothers?
I do not know who I am.

I am not a Christian, a Jew, a Magian, or a Muslim.
I am not of the East, the West, the land, or the sea.
I was not formed by Nature, nor by the circling heavens;
    Not by earth, nor water, nor air, nor fire.

I am not the king nor the beggar;
    Not of substance nor of form.
I am not from India, China, nor a bordering country;
    Not from Persia, nor the lands of Khorasan.
I am not of this world nor the next;
    Not of heaven nor of hell.

I came not from Adam nor from Eve;
I do not dwell in Eden nor the gardens of paradise;
My place is placeless, my trace is traceless.
Nothing is mine, neither body nor soul—
    All belongs to the heart of my Beloved.

I have cast away all differences,
    and now see the two worlds as one.
I call, I seek, I know, I am only one.

Now I know you and you alone.
Drunk from the wine of Love's cup,
    the two worlds have slipped from my reach.

I have nothing left to do here
    save drink your wine
    and dance with delight.

If one moment passes without you,
    from then on my life
    will be worthless.

If once in my life I get a glimpse of you
I will trample down both worlds,
    dancing in triumph forever.

O Shams,
    I am so drunk on your love
    I have lost this entire world.

Besides the sweet taste of your wine
    I have no tale left to tell.

A GARDEN BEYOND PARADISE

Everything you see has its roots
    in the Unseen world.
The forms may change,
    yet the essence remains the same.

Every wondrous sight will vanish,
Every sweet word will fade.
    But do not be disheartened,
The Source they come from is eternal—
Growing, branching out,
    giving new life and new joy.

Why do you weep?—
That Source is within you,
And this whole world
    is springing up from it.

The Source is full,
Its waters are ever-flowing;
    Do not grieve,
      drink your fill!
Don't think it will ever run dry—
This is the endless Ocean!

From the moment you came into this world
A ladder was placed in front of you
    that you might escape.

From earth you became plant,
From plant you became animal.

Afterwards you became a human being,
Endowed with knowledge, intellect, and faith.

Behold the body, born of dust—
how perfect it has become!

Why should you fear its end?
When were you ever made less by dying?

When you pass beyond this human form,
No doubt you will become an angel
And soar through the heavens!

But don't stop there.
Even heavenly bodies grow old.

Pass again from the heavenly realm
and plunge into the vast ocean of Consciousness.
Let the drop of water that is you
become a hundred mighty seas.

But do not think that the drop alone
Becomes the Ocean—
the Ocean, too, becomes the drop!

GLOSSARY OF TERMS

BRAHMIN'S THREAD: A small string worn by Brahmins—the religious class of Indian society—as part of a boy's initiation into manhood.

DARVESH: (Lit. "poor man"); one who calls nothing his own. One engaged in spiritual practice under the guidance of a *Shaykh* or spiritual Master; a member of a Sufi order. Also spelled *dervish*.

KA'BE: The cubed-shaped Muslim shrine at Mecca that encloses the sacred black stone given to Abraham by the angel Gabriel. Muslim worshipers always face the *Ka'be* while praying.

KHEZR: The prophet or sage who became immortal by drinking from the water of life. Khezr is the patron saint of wandering seekers who mysteriously appears in order to guide them, protect them, and in rare instances, initiate them into the Sufi path. Also known as Khidr.

KONYA: A city in present-day Turkey where Rumi lived most of his life, and where his mausoleum is located.

KORAN: The sacred book of the Muslims containing the revelations of Muhammad.

MAGIAN: One of the Magi. The priestly caste of ancient Persia who considered fire to be the purest and most noble of elements, and fit to worship as a form of God. They were "the wise men from the East" mentioned in the Gospels.

MAULANA: (Lit. "Our Master"). The name by which Rumi was most commonly addressed by his disciples.

MECCA: The holy city of Islam that contains the *Ka'be;* birthplace of Muhammad and the most famous pilgrimage site for Muslims.

MEVLEVI: The Sufi order known in the West as "The Whirling Dervishes." This order was inspired by Rumi and its name comes from the Turkish pronunciation for *Maulana* ("Our Master"), a title given to Rumi.

OXUS RIVER: An old name for the Amu Darya River which runs along the border of USSR and Afghanistan.

PARANDA: (Lit. "Bird"). The nickname given to Shams, who was often reported as being in two distant cities on the same day.

PRAYER ROCK: A small rock used by Muslims during prayers to mark the position where the head must touch in order to face the *Ka'be* in Mecca.

(THE) PROPHET: Muhammad; founder of the Muslim faith.

RAMADAN: The ninth month of the Muslim calendar in which the faithful fast each day from sunrise to sunset.

RUBA'I: From the Arabic meaning "foursome," it is a four line poem (quatrain), of Persian origin, with the first, second, and fourth hemistiches rhyming. Plural: *ruba'iyat.*

RUBAAB: A stringed instrument that is often played with a bow.

SAAQI: A beautiful maiden who pours wine. Symbolically she represents divine grace, the form of the Beloved who intoxicates the soul by pouring the wine of love. This reference comes from the Koran which describes God as, "He who gives to drink."

SA'MAA: (Lit: "audition"). The sacred whirling dance of the darveshes, where the motions of the human body represent the movements
of the universe. The term also refers to any Sufi practice that involves
music and chanting.

SHAMS-E TABRIZ: ("The Glorious Sun of Tabriz"). Rumi's spiritual master who came from Tabriz, an ancient city in northwest Iran.
Also: *Shamsuddin, Shams Din, Shams.*

SHAYKH: A spiritual master of the Islamic tradition.

SULTAN WALAD: Rumi's eldest son who formally established the
Mevlevi Order of Whirling Dervishes.

SUFI: From the Arabic root (*suf*) "wool," referring to the wool
garments that were worn by the earliest Sufis; but also from (*safa*),
"purity." A Sufi is a member of the mystical order of Islam based on
love and devotion.

TURNING WORLDS: The constant movement of the universe;
the natural movement in the process of creation.

TWO WORLDS: Heaven and earth. This world and the next.

WATER OF LIFE: The nectar of immortality; the life-giving water
of God; the primordial waters of creation.

SUFI SYMBOLISM

BELOVED: God and His loving aspects which are accessible to man's immediate experience. Also: *Lover, Sweetheart.*

BREEZE: The life-giving breath of the Beloved.

BUBBLE: Individual existence. Man is a bubble compared to the ocean (God). See *foam.*

BURNING: Process of purification of the soul.

CROW: A dark or negative force that often surrounds the soul.

DRUNKENNESS: Divine intoxication; a soul enraptured with the love of God.

FACE: God's true form, one not covered by the veils of the world.

FALCON: The soul, often portrayed as trapped in this physical world longing for the wrist of the King (God).

FOAM: Outward and shallow forms (of limited existence) that cover the depths of the infinite ocean (God).

GARDEN: The beauty and bliss of Paradise; a symbol for God's creative power. The place in this world (or the next) where lovers come into the presence of the Beloved.

GREAT BIRD: The transcendent nature of God, the One who can fly anywhere.

HAIR: The power of illusion, *Maya.* Also tresses, curls, or lockets.

IMPOSTER: The aspect of God that tricks the soul into thinking the world is real.

KILLING: The destruction of one's ego and its limited sense of identity. It especially refers to the breaking of one's attachment to the physical body. The Persian word is *fana,* most commonly translated as "annihilation."

KING: God; an epithet for the Beloved.

LANGUAGE OF THE BIRDS: Words of the spirit that transcend the limits of this world.

NIGHTINGALE: The soul longing for the Beloved or His eternal beauty (represented by the rose).

OCEAN: God. The universe.

PEARL: The perfection and beauty of one's true self. Divine wisdom.

ROSE: The eternal and perfect beauty of the Beloved.

ROSE GARDEN: Paradise and its eternal beauty.

WEDDING NIGHT: The night the soul (lover) joins in union with God (the Beloved). It also refers to the day a great saint leaves this world.

WINE: Nectar; the intoxicating love of God.

VERSES OF THE PROPHET

These are lines found in the Koran (revelations of the Prophet) and the Traditions (sayings attributed to the Prophet), which are commonly cited by the Sufis, and upon which the core of their teachings are based.

FROM THE KORAN

To God belongs the East and the West; in whatever direction you turn to look, there is the Face of God. (2:115)

To God we belong, and unto Him we shall return. (2:156)

If my servants ask about me, tell them surely, I am near. (2:186)

The seven heavens, the earth, and every creature who dwells therein proclaims the glory of God. There is not a thing that does not celebrate His glory. (17:44)

There is no god other than Him. Everything will perish except His Face. (28:88)

[Solomon] said: "O people! We have been taught the language of the birds, and on us He has bestowed all gifts. Indeed this is Grace." (27:16)

God's will is ever done. (22:18)

Life in this world is but play and amusement. (47:36)

We (God) created man, and We know the dark yearnings of his soul. For We are nearer to him than his jugular vein. (50:16)

On earth there are signs for those of true faith, and also in your own Selves. Why do you not see? (51:20–21)

I have created man and spirits for one reason—that they may worship Me. (51:56)

FROM THE TRADITIONS

I was a Hidden Treasure and I wished to be known. Therefore I created the world that I might be known.

Truly, my mercy takes precedence over my wrath.

God is beautiful and He loves beauty.

In the heart of man lies the Throne of God.

No one shall meet God who has not first met His Messenger.

Whoever knows himself, knows his Lord.

BIBLIOGRAPHY

PRIMARY SOURCE

Furuzanfar, Badi-uz-Zaman. *Kulliyat-e Shams.* Tehran: Amir Kabir Press, 1957–66; Tehran: University of Tehran, 1963, Vol. 8.

SOURCES CONSULTED

Aflaki, Shems al Din Ahmad. *Menaaquibu al Arifin,* trans., James Redhouse, *Legends of the Sufis.* Wheaton, IL: The Theosophical Publishing House, 1976.

Arberry, A. J. trans., *Mystical Poems of Rumi.* Chicago: University of Chicago Press, 1968.

_____. trans., *Mystical Poems of Rumi 2.* Chicago: University of Chicago Press, 1991.

_____. *Sufism: An Account of the Mystics of Islam.* London: George Allen and Unwin, 1968.

Baldick, Julian. *Mystical Islam: An Introduction to Sufism.* New York: New York University Press, 1980.

Behari, Bankey. *Sufis, Mystics, and Yogis of India.* Bombay: Bharatiya Vidya Bhavan, 1962.

Chittick, William. *The Sufi Path of Love.* Albany: SUNY Press, 1983.

Dermenghem, Emile. *Muhammad and the Islamic Tradition,* trans., Jean M. Watt. Woodstock, NY: The Overlook Press, 1981.

Friedlander, Ira. *The Whirling Dervishes*. Albany: SUNY Press, 1991.

Goldin, Marylin. "Love is the Flame which Burns Everything." *Darshan Magazine,* vol. 14, pp. 71–84; and vol. 15, pp. 79–85.

Helminski, Edmund. *The Ruins of the Heart*. Putney, VT: Threshold Books, 1981.

Hakim, Khalifa Abdul. *The Metaphysics of Rumi*. Lahore: Institute of Islamic Culture, 1977.

Iqbal, Afzal. *The Life and Work of Jalaluddin Rumi*. London: Octagon Press, 1983.

Iqbal, Muhammad. *The Development of Metaphysics in Persia*. London: Luzac and Co., 1908.

Khosla, K. *The Sufism of Rumi*. Longmead, UK: Element Books Ltd., 1987.

Moyne, John and Barks, Coleman. *Open Secret*. Putney, VT: Threshold Books, 1984.

_____. *Unseen Rain: Quatrains of Rumi*. Putney, VT: Threshold Books, 1986.

Muehleisen-Arnold, John. *The Koran and the Bible*. London: Longmans, Green, Reader, and Dyer, 1866.

Nicholson, R. A. *The Mystics of Islam*. New York: Shocken Books, 1975.

_____. trans., *Rumi: Divani Shams Tabriz*. San Francisco: The Rainbow Bridge, 1973.

_____. *Translations of Eastern Poetry and Prose*. New York: Greenwood Press, 1969.

Schimmel, Annemarie. *Mystical Dimensions of Islam.* Chapel Hill: University of North Carolina Press, 1975.

_____. *The Triumphal Sun.* London: East-West Publications, 1978.

Stoddard, William. *Sufism.* New York: Paragon House, 1978.

Ullah, Najib, ed., *Islamic Literature.* New York: Washington Square Press, 1963.

Vitray-Meyerovitch, Eva de. *Rumi and Sufism,* trans., Simone Fattal. Sausalito, CA: The Post-Apollo Press, 1987.

Whinfield, E. H. *Teachings of Rumi.* London: Octagon Press, 1979.

Williams, John A. *Islam.* New York: George Braziller, 1962.

Wilson, Peter L. and Pourjavady, Nasrollah. *The Drunken Universe.* Grand Rapids, MI: Phanes Press, 1987.

TEXT REFERENCES

The numbers below refer to the assignment found in the Kulliyat-e
Shams, *edited by B. Z. Furuzanfar, Amir Kabir Press edition, unless
followed by "t" which refers to the assignment found in the University of Tehran edition. The symbol "(??)" refers to those quatrains
that are commonly attributed to Rumi but not found in either
Furuzanfar edition.*

QUATRAINS

The Beloved (p. 3)
1408, 238, 55, 511, 80, 285, 784, 569, 910, 428, 1474, 797t, (??), 956,
193, 720, 942t, 983, 334, 454, 839t, 208, 64, 1344, 926, 1330, 1318, 832,
479t, 1332, 858, 268, 863, 297, 1019t, 1035, 749, 1169, 245t.

The Sufi Path (p. 25)
91, 848, 464, 831, 280, 674, 1464, 735t, 1313, 153, 729, 805, 1348t, 1315,
101t, 358, 1188t, 773, 263, 830, 435, 859, 405t, 686, 1091, 816, 834t, 662,
1022.

Divine Intoxication (p. 37)
684, 1306, 926, 1431, 1159, 97, 670, 802, 904, 629t, 1050, 261, 470, 1164,
823, 567.

Teachings (p. 47)
84, 598, 393, 230, 305, 369, 768t, 1228, 77, 1504, 1237t, 1238t, 1239t,
1246, 1129, 593, 745t, 551, 1798, 775, 719t, 827, 1246.

The Heart-Ravishing Beloved (p. 61)
557t, 1854, 533, 1080, 677, 210, 650, 809, 1279, 1287, 1044, 269, 1230,
1175, 490, 735, 1076, 681, 1359, 1087, 742t, 911, 1128, 340, 1115, 276,
1118t, 912, 430, 1312, 161, 368, 361.

Union (The Wedding Night) (p. 79)
168, 1029, 531, 511, 604, 754, 287, 1652, 1208, 1526, 973, (??), 203,
1149t, 565, 776t, 1242, 309, 45, 1249.

ODES

*The numbers below refer to the assignment found in the Furuzanfar
edition of* Kulliyat-e Shams, *unless preceded by "N," which refers
to the assignment found in R. A. Nicholson's* Selected Poems from
the Divani Shamsi Tabriz. *Entries marked with an asterisk were
rendered by Jonathan Star from previous translations of Nicholson
and Arberry. 1, 36, 37, 406, 442, 1529, 451, 457, 505, 598*, 881,
929, 1081, 1502, 1603, 1634*, 1658, 1668, 1919*, N8*, 1937*, 2037,
2131, 2138, 2209, 2214, 3296, 3365, 3401, N31*, N12*.*

ABOUT THE TRANSLATORS

JONATHAN STAR graduated from Harvard University with honors where he studied Eastern Religion and architecture. For the last fifteen years he has studied with various Zen and Yogic Masters including Swami Muktananda and Gurumayi Chidvilasananda. His poetry and writings have been translated into several languages and his works include a translation of the *Tao Te Ching,* and *Two Suns Rising: A Collection of Sacred Writings* (Bantam Books). He divides his time between New York City and Princeton, New Jersey.

SHAHRAM SHIVA was born in Mashhad, Khorasan (Iran), and comes from a long line of Persian poets. He is a clothing designer, artist, and photographer. For the last seven years he has practiced Siddha Yoga and various Sufi disciplines, including the whirling dance of the dirveshes. He lives in New York City.